# Under His Shadow
*my journey*

## Sarah J. Wessels

SARAH J. WESSELS

*All rights reserved. This publication or parts thereof may not be reproduced in any form, stored in a retrieval system, or transmitted in any form by any means — electronic, mechanical, photocopy, recording, or otherwise -without prior written permission of the publisher.*

*Sarah@UnderHisShadow.me*
*www.UnderHisShadow.me*

*Cover designed by Lawrence Edge*

*ISBN 978-0-6921-1327-1*
*Library of Congress Control Number 2018905708*

*"He who dwells in the secret place of the Most High shall abide under the shadow of the Almighty."*

Psalm 91:1 (NKJV)

# Dedication

I dedicate this to:

My Heavenly Father, Jesus and Holy Spirit. Your love transformed my life! Without You I could not do anything. You carried me through all my life and watched over me. You are faithful, kind, compassionate, awesome God!

My mother, whose faithfulness and gentle encouragement guided my life from the beginning. You never stopped praying for me, believing in me. You were my inspiration when I needed it most. Thank you, Mom!

My amazing three daughters, Marguerite, Lisl and Landi. Your love and support in times when I could not face anymore tomorrows were the reason for me not to give up.

# Endorsements:

Sarah shares openly and honestly with readers about the joys and struggles of her life, growing up on a farm in South Africa. This led her into a deep belief that she was shy and insignificant. This caused her to make many devastating decisions that adversely affected her life and the lives of her children, and no matter how hard she tried, she was constantly overcome with stress and defeat. Then one day that all changed.. she came into an intimate relationship with Jesus Christ and learned how to rest in His presence. This enabled her to learn to "let go and let God do it". You will read about how then and only then was the Holy Spirit able to reveal to her the deep issues of her heart, heal her and set her free. Her book will inspire you and encourage you, that God can and will bring his amazing victory also into your life.
John Arnott, Catch the Fire Ministries, Toronto

It is not often that the story of God's faithfulness and provision will move my soul to the point of tears, but Sarah's life and choices did so. This book is a testimony of her willingness to surrender to the fierce love of her Heavenly Father and find hope and victory in Him. You will, no doubt, identify with many of her struggles but may also find the same life giving answers.
Jeremy Sinnott, Pastor, Catch the Fire Ministries

This is absolutely stunning work. I am so blessed to have shared in your journey. Reading, I often felt I was sitting with you on the porch or in the living room. You lean forward and bring out the finest treasures of your heart and the Lord's, and we both tear up. I savored every word and drank deeply of the wisdom from your faith walk. Thank you for letting me linger with you and listen to your beautiful voice. These pages are alive with hope and saturated in the Lord's Presence. Thank

you for the rich encouragement and for sharing so openly. Your story penetrates the heart, calls forth identity and destiny, and shines as a lighthouse that will lead many home.
Joan Hutter, Women Abide

Across the world, we are hoping to have our Voice heard. Sarah brings a raw and open story of her life that challenges others that THEIR voice also matters. This trail of the Love and Faithfulness of God rings loud and clear that He is with us and for us at every turn. Her writing crosses all barriers of language and culture as she speaks from the language of the heart. This is a fantastic, and very practical read and we can anticipate many other books from within the well that Sarah draws from!
Karen Machovina

The one consistent memory I have of growing up is listening to my mom as she tells us Bible stories. She taught me that Jesus loves us, and she demonstrated His love to us by the way she loves us. As Abraham Lincoln said: "I remember my mother's prayers and they have always followed me. They have clung to me all my life". She never gave up, even when life was so hard. She always gave us the best she could and made sure we never went without. Only now I realize just how much she gave up so that we could be blessed. Even now she continues to teach me how to be the best mom I can be by the way she lives, the way she treats my children and the way she treats my husband and me, the way she treats others. Her best quality is her humility and her pure love for people and, most of all, her love for our Heavenly Father. I am proud to be called Sarah's daughter.
Lisl Budfuloski

Looking back, I only realize now as a parent myself how difficult it must have been to raise all of us by herself, especially in the circumstances that she did. My mom is an incredible woman! I am so proud of her, not only for raising

three daughters by herself but to do so with grace, patience and a whole lot of love in some very difficult times. I'm grateful for how she allowed the Lord the work in her heart and thankful for all He's done in her and now doing through her. Her words of wisdom guide me and I am so incredibly grateful for her impact in my husband and my children's lives and my own. I am honored to call her Mom.
Landi Odendaal

    Sarah is a remarkable woman of God. The way my mom carefully stewards Truth from the Word has deeply impacted my life. The Lord has completely transformed her life. She is a testimony of Jesus' covering of our shame and restoring our honor. She is life giving to those around her. The Lord uses her tenderness and strength in Him to bring down many walls in peoples' lives and see them walk in freedom. We've ministered together internationally and much fruit has come from her ministry. She is "Mama" to many who have received healing through her ministry. What the Lord did for our family, He can do for you. This book is filled with keys to freedom, building faith and trusting in Him. I've seen my mother's walk from victim to victorious, from brokenness to being able to help others. I highly recommend this book.
Marguerite Evans
*Marguerite Evans Ministries*

# Acknowledgements

My book would not be complete without Marguerite asking countless questions, giving advice, and helping with direction, which helped my 17 page story grow. Also Lisl and Landi helping me on the computer, encouraging me. Thank you for coming to my rescue many times, thank you for all your reading!

My dear friend, Karen Machovina who are such a blessing to me. Thank you for all your help and encouragement. Your input made me excited to continue with my story.

A very special thank you to Lawrence and Barbara Edge who saw the heart of my book. Thank you for spending so many hours in editing and the designing of my cover page. It touched my heart! I appreciate you and I thank the Lord for you!

I am forever grateful to John and Carol Arnott from Catch the Fire Ministries. They shared about the Father's Love even before the 1994 Revival. The Revival is also known as the "Father's Blessing". The fruit of their desperate pursuit of more of the Lord (and the powerful move of the Holy Spirit) was the rescue of me and my daughters. We were all so incredibly broken.

We learned from them how to pursue Him, how to increase hunger for more of Him and how to rest in the Lord's Presence. Today we know that our Heavenly Father loves us deeply and cares for us. Jesus truly is alive and transforms lives. Because of the price John and Carol paid, and because of the hunger for more of the Lord that our pastor, Ed Roebert in South Africa had, we are who we are today. Pastor Ed Roebert is now with the Lord. I thank the Lord for these people who said "yes" to the call God had on their lives.

I particularly want to honor and thank all those, unnamed, who have been obedient to the God of Salvation in helping myself and my daughters along the way. Without you we would not have made it this far, and there would be no book to read.

# Foreword

When I met Sarah Wessels, my first impression was one of a well-groomed, confident, attractive woman in good health and still enjoying the "youth of old age". I couldn't have known that what I was seeing was refined gold, the end-product of a life spent dwelling under the shadow of the Almighty. This life's-tale is a story, not only of God's redemption, but of overcoming some of modern life's most insurmountable obstacles by continuing in His shadow. It's the story of a painfully shy little girl, one of the daughters of a humble, hard-working South African farmer who, himself, found strength and self-confidence elusive, a little girl who would one day be the mother helping her (former beauty queen) daughter bring the message of Jesus' love to oppressed women in some of the world's darkest corners.

Sarah became a teacher, a Christian leader, and at times an international speaker proclaiming the message of God's unfailing faithfulness, gained from a life that proved it. Her present efforts, including writing this book, are pointed toward revealing the pathway to overcoming unwarranted fear, lack of self-confidence, and the lie of personal worthlessness.

She has found strength without losing the virtue of humility. In a way, she's once again the little girl under a blanket in her secret place, a raging African thunderstorm roaring outside, unable to disturb the sweet comfort of His presence…this time, inviting us to join her.

She's not forgotten the story of both where she came from and how she got where she is, and she has done a fine job of putting it on paper in English, her second language. Enjoy.

Lawrence Edge

# Contents

| | | |
|---|---|---|
| Chapter 1 | Life on a South African farm | 17 |
| Chapter 2 | A thing called school | 25 |
| Chapter 3 | The small house | 31 |
| Chapter 4 | Unfulfilled dreams | 35 |
| Chapter 5 | The wonder of family | 41 |
| Chapter 6 | Party time! | 45 |
| Chapter 7 | Farmgirl / Citygirl | 49 |
| Chapter 8 | Brokenness in school | 53 |
| Chapter 9 | Step without faith | 57 |
| Chapter 10 | My daughters, my treasures | 63 |
| Chapter 11 | The God of miracles! | 67 |
| Chapter 12 | The one horse town | 71 |
| Chapter 13 | A letter and a dream | 77 |
| Chapter 14 | The new South Africa | 81 |
| Chapter 15 | Making ends meet | 87 |
| Chapter 16 | Rest, Rest, Rest! | 93 |
| Chapter 17 | Toronto! | 101 |
| Chapter 18 | My first son! | 105 |
| Chapter 19 | Opportunity of a lifetime | 111 |
| Chapter 20 | Reality back home | 121 |
| Chapter 21 | "Life and death is in the power of the tongue" | 125 |
| Chapter 22 | Wedding in the mountains! | 129 |
| Chapter 23 | Wedding via skype! | 133 |
| Chapter 24 | In a place of transition | 135 |
| Chapter 25 | God is faithful! | 139 |
| Chapter 26 | I have a voice | 141 |

# CHAPTER 1

## *Life on a South African farm*

*"For I know the plans I have for you, declares the Lord.*
*Plans to prosper you and not to harm you.*
*Plans to give you Hope and a future."*
Jeremiah 29:11

I grew up on a farm in the late 40s and 1950s in South Africa, the eldest of four daughters. It was a time before paved roads, when deep blue African skies were yet uncluttered with the white sky-trails left by commercial airliners, and abundant wildlife was still holding its own in seemingly endless numbers across the continent.

We had an old house built from sandstone with a spacious verandah and a lovely view of the fields and the surrounding area. As small children we loved playing with our dolls on that verandah—also watching the ants coming out of the cracks in the concrete floor. I was always amazed at the way they gathered food and how busy they were.

As I grew up, in a world where nature was at my fingertips every day and such an important part of life, it was easy for this child to understand what was meant by Proverbs 6:6-8: *"Go to the ant you sluggard. Consider its ways and be wise. It has no commander. No overseer or ruler. Yet it stores its provisions in summer and gathers its food at harvest."*

In those days, electric power had not yet reached the farms, and we had to depend on candles and paraffin lamps for light. We had to be very careful walking with the candles while they changed the atmosphere in the house into a mysterious world of light and shadows.

I still remember how dark the nights could be if there was no moonlight coming through the windows. For me it was very scary, and many times I fell asleep with the blankets over my head.

There was a big black coal stove that added so much character and warmth to the house. The kitchen was the place where we, as a family, gathered during the cold winter evenings. First thing in the morning my mother would take out the ashes and light a new fire.

The smell of freshly baked bread, coupled with the aroma of the big coffeepot on the stove, is something I'll always remember. The more even, when I think about all the wonderful meals that were cooked on that stove.

During Christmas seasons, homemade cookies were added to the list of these precious memories. How I treasure the memory of the excitement of waiting for the cookies to be ready—and then eating handfuls of them.
Life was not easy; my father had to work very hard. There were no tractors. He had to make use of oxen pulling the implements. Everything was hard labor and took nearly his every waking hour. It was normal for those farmers to start working when it was still dark and work until close to midnight, just to start again after only a few hours of sleep.

My paternal grandparents lived on the farm next to us. Their house was within walking distance of ours.
Our grandmother was a very special person. She was always kind and ready to help wherever there was a need.

What we surely enjoyed was her home-baked bread served with fresh cream instead of butter. That was a real treat for us, enough reason for a daily visit!

Her good heart was not only for people, her chickens also benefitted from it. Between the two houses was the family graveyard. For some reason, her hen made a nest for herself and her little chicks in the grass between the graves.

One night there was a huge storm. In the midst of that, grandmother went all by herself to rescue them. When I heard about it I could not believe it; I still think she was very brave!

Then there were the long summer days melting into evenings and nights that seemed to be owned by millions of unseen insects, all loudly calling at the same time.
Many times at bedtime we could see lightning in the distance. My dad would usually tell us at what time we could expect the rain to come.

Usually the first raindrops would wake me up. The storm would start with soft uneven drops, falling harder and harder on the metal roof until they exploded into a raging thunderstorm. There's nothing like an African thunderstorm! It is like the roar of a lion, you feel it in your bones! Lightning lit up the whole house. It was such an amazing, peaceful feeling listening to the rain while curled up underneath the blankets. I was not afraid of the thunder. I knew God was in it, as my Mother told us. He is so mighty, I didn't have to fear. Eventually I would fall asleep, waking up the next morning with everything outside fresh and clean. Even the birds in the surrounding trees sounded more cheerful!

We used to visit our neighbors in the evenings. The roads between the farms were narrow and sandy. In the rainy season it could be very slippery. When we came back late in the evening, everything was so quiet and peaceful, covered in moonlight. The only noise was the sound of the engine of the car. Inside, everybody was quiet, some children having fallen asleep.

Every now and then a rabbit would run into the road, totally confused by the lights shining on him.

At last the little animal would realize that freedom is so close, just a jump away, beside the road. At the speed of light he would then disappear into the grass in the dark.

I always stared at the stars through the window of the car. They looked so bright and close in the African sky. I thought heaven must be somewhere between them, a wonderful place to be.

For the first few years of my life our transport was a horse and cart. It took us hours to visit my maternal grandparents, although they were not far away. My mom and dad sat on the front seat with me sitting behind them, on the backseat. Although the horses were well fed, I always felt sorry for them and I can still hear the rhythmic fall of their hooves on the dirt road.

Many normal everyday things that we take for granted now were a luxury for us back then. Living on a farm gave us all the essential things we needed like fresh meat, eggs, vegetables, milk and cream. Because of this, my beautiful mother would even make our own butter. She also made us cold drinks, and that is why we were not concerned about hailstorms, because for a few minutes we could have natural ice cubes in our cold drinks—very fascinating for us!

My parents couldn't afford things like Coca Cola and chocolates, which were only for special occasions. But there was, however, a little farm shop close by with lots of cheap sweeties, and those were a special treat for us!

There were no supermarkets where you could take your trolley and walk through all the different aisles. There was no opportunity to compare prices or brands. You would take your grocery list and give it to the assistant behind the counter and she would get everything for you. There were no credit or debit cards, you could only pay cash.

Life was simple, and there were no TVs. When we would get visitors, the children played games outside, playing with a ball, running and chasing each other. We had so much fun while the adults were together. They sometimes had coffee at the big dining room table, talking for hours. The men would share their experiences on the farm—what harvest they expected and always about the weather. The women's favorite topics were their children and the sharing of recipes and knitting patterns.

Usually the visitors would stay over for a meal and we could have a nice *braai* (barbecue) outside. Nobody was in a hurry, and it was safe to travel home late night all by yourself, by foot or maybe by horse.

My mother made all of our clothes and knitted us beautiful jerseys. I loved going to town, which meant I had a ribbon perfectly tied in my hair. Ribbons were fashionable. Whether you had long or short hair, a fancy colored ribbon was part of the hairstyle.

Buying new shoes was an important day in our lives. Wow! New white or black shiny shoes! Just the thought of it made us so excited that we could hardly wait to get to town. In those days we only had one pair of shoes, maybe a pair of sandals and a pair of slippers. Later, school shoes were added. A new dress or new shoes could bring us so much joy!

Because there was also no computers or video games, we had to keep ourselves busy in more traditional ways. We loved playing "house" with our dolls. We even had paper dolls. It was easy to make them clothes; that kept us busy for hours!

Not many people had radios, but we had one. It was huge and because there was no electricity, it was powered by a car battery. The reception was not always good. I remember when Afrikaans folk music played, my favorite spot was on the floor in front of the radio. For some reason that kind of music made me cry. I could not stop crying! Music was the voice through which the culture was heard, and something in the sound touched my heart in a way that I could not understand.

When there was an important rugby match, our neighbors, Uncle Barry and Aunt Lulu, would visit to listen with my parents to the broadcast on the radio. I could never understand why people running after a ball could give them so much joy! They were always so excited, jumping and shouting when there was a score for their team!

One day I decided to make my mom tea. The huge kettle with water was boiling on the stove. I don't know what happened, but my younger sister was in my way and I accidentally spilled boiling water over her arm. I felt so bad about that. It also seemed more serious to me because she had to wear a bandage on her arm. Somehow Aunt Lulu heard about the incident.

On the day of her unexpected visit my sister and I were sitting close together at the back of the house when she came around the corner. I can still see the tall figure with her long dress and her grey hair in a bun coming towards us. She was pointing her finger at me angrily saying, "Don't you ever play with boiling water again!" With her harsh tone her words pierced my heart. She turned around and walked into the house, leaving me with a very painful, guilty feeling. Her words had a deep effect on my life. Because I could not face her again until she left, I decided to hide from her 'til I was sure she was gone. I felt so lonely and hurt by this angry woman.

After all, I only wanted to surprise my mom with a cup of tea. Moments like these can affect us all our lives, even into adulthood, as it did for me.

The feeling of hopelessness and guilt when you tried to do something special and you end up hurting someone by accident. In that moment I had no voice.

Deep inside there was the knowing that our parents loved us and would do everything possible for their children. I can't remember much of the first few years of my life except that my mother was my everything, and to this day we are very close. Sometimes the neighbors' children would come to play with my dolls. There was no way they could change the clothes that were sewn onto them, and if they wanted to, they had to put different clothes over the clothes my mother had chosen. We loved playing outside. We spent our time making furniture and houses for our dolls using grass and little sticks—totally different from today's magnificent toyshops!

# CHAPTER 2

## *A thing called school*

Until the age of seven my mother home-schooled me. After that I went to a little school on a farm that was close by. Together with a few other children, my school transport was the back car of a freight train. We had to sit on the floor between barrels of cream. I thought it would be fun going to school by train but it was not. I had so much fear. Not only could I miss the steps while jumping onto the slow-moving train, but I was afraid of one of the big boys who took pleasure in teasing me. He threatened that he was going to throw me off of the train.

In my imagination I could feel this big black engine driving over me, turning me into nothing. Luckily it was a short distance from one station to the next. Not only was this trip uncomfortable, but, judging by the smell, one could tell that the previous passengers had been some pigs! It was not nice and clean or meant for the transport of people.

When getting off the train, we still had a half an hour walk to the school. It was a gravel road and sometimes a vehicle would pass. Not everybody was sensitive for the few school children walking in the road. Many times my black and white school outfit was covered with dust. You could even taste the dust!

After school we had to wait for a few hours for the late afternoon passenger train. On this train we also sat on the floor at the back. While waiting for the train, the other children would play around the station, but I would sit on my little suitcase, tired and lonely, wishing for the train to come. In my heart I longed to be part of them, but something was holding me back. I did not have the confidence to join them. Deep inside there was a fear that they would not want me to join them. The safest thing to do was just to sit on my own, waiting for the train to come.

My mother did a good job of teaching me during those first two years at home, but nobody realized that this little girl was emotionally not ready for a thing called school. I was so secure in my little world with my parents and sisters. I had very little experience playing with other children and now, all of a sudden, it was not only the train and the school, but there were more new and frightening experiences. I was not used to being away from my family for most of the day. I was so confused! In spite of all this, the principal decided that I was intellectually ready to join the next class, in which I was a year younger than the rest of the pupils.

In school I didn't talk to anybody. I just smiled and wanted to please everyone. When standing in a row at the teacher's table, I would keep on giving my place to the other children. I thought I was doing them a favor. Never did I realize that this could be the beginning of a lifestyle. My heart was for others to be blessed, but, as I was to learn later in life, when graciousness comes from an insecure, unhealed place, what one might have meant as a blessing could simply make the giver miss opportunities and hold him or her back.

The school had two teachers, two classrooms, a big yard and a donkey. When he was bored, the donkey would come to the school building. He liked watching us through the windows. He also liked the sandwiches the children generously shared with him!

We were four different grades in one class, with a total of about 15 pupils. Everything was new to me. I had no friends. During breaks I sat outside all by myself, eating my sandwiches.

Although my teacher was very kind, she did not try to connect me with the other children. The only time that I was part of the game was when they played a certain ball game. There was a huge rock in the schoolyard and they loved making two teams, throwing the ball over the rock to each other. I remember enjoying that game.

My parents didn't know what was going on. There was a huge emotional gap between me and the other children—something that would cause me so much pain and rejection, lasting for many years into adulthood.

My train experience only lasted for a while. My aunt who lived close to the school asked me to come and stay with them, which meant I would be at home only on the weekends.

I cried so much. What made it worse was that my cousin could be very nasty to me. She was a year older than me. She did not want me to play with her dolls. I had to pretend an empty bottle was a doll.

One day my dad bought me a beautiful doll. Guess what happened? She decided to play with my new doll and then gave me one of her old dolls to play with. I did not say anything. I could not stand up for myself. My uncle, my aunt and my cousin lived in a house at the foot of a hill. It was close to the school. My cousin and I loved playing with our dolls (or my bottle!) in the grass in front of the house. My aunt did not like gardening, therefore the grass was always long.

In winter, this house was like a modern day freezer—ice-cold! Because of a big coal stove, the kitchen was always nice and warm. But opening the door to the rest of the house was another story. It felt as if the cold was hurting you!

There was no running water in the bathroom. In the morning my aunt would bring us some hot water in a bowl. My cousin always had the chance to wash herself first while I was standing

there, on my cousin's command, in my underwear, waiting for her to finish. And she took her time, not caring about me standing shivering from the cold. One day my grandmother was visiting and she quickly made an end to that.
Sometimes in the afternoons we would each take a huge grain bag and go to the surrounding fields. We would then start gathering bones from animals that had died. After a few days we would take our harvest to the little shop close by.

Mr. Muller, the owner, was an elderly German man. He always bought our bones and gave us some cash for it. He would then send them to be ground up and used again. Most of the time we would spend our money right there in the shop. Mr. Muller always had special sweeties we really liked!

After two years, I went to the other class. I was so scared of our teacher, Mr. van Zyl. Somehow he realized that I could not see properly. As a result of that, I had to wear glasses. I still remember those funny glasses with the small round lenses. I was so self-conscious to go to school. In my imagination I could see everybody laughing at me.

On the first morning I wore my glasses, when the bell rang for the school to start, we all lined up in two rows in front of the school. I was so self-conscious it was difficult for me to go to school that Monday morning. But nobody laughed. They were just staring at me. Maybe Mr. van Zyl had something to do with that. What a relief that was!

We always knew our home was a safe place. My father was big and tall. His self-confidence gave us so much security. We knew we had nothing to fear when he was near.

My mother, on the other hand, made sure that not only our physical needs, like having clothes, were met, but she also took care of the spiritual needs we had as well. She was the one who read to us from the Bible and taught us how to pray. My favorite story was about Lazarus and the rich man. I wanted to listen to it over and over!

I think what touched me the most at that young age was that poor Lazarus was happy now and would never be hungry again.

Unlike my sisters who were always playing, running, laughing and turning the house upside-down, I preferred my own company. When we were reading, I was reading the Bible. Sunday afternoons was a time of rest for the family and I would sit at the dining room table, reading my Bible. I also had my own secret way that I could escape into a world of my own—a world where I was happy. In spite of my fears, I had a world that brought me much joy, especially since Jesus was part of it. He was with me, choosing me as His favorite. He was always so kind and loving.

I sometimes took my secret to school, and, although in the company of other children, I could easily be in faraway places. Even in high school, especially when a class was boring, I was gone in moments! Looking back, I don't know how I made it through the Typewriting class during my final school year. While typing, my imagination tours were on-the-go, and I still received 'A' results. For me it was unbelievable!

I was not only a dreamer, I was also shy in an extreme way. When I was small and there were visitors, I would always hide behind my mother's dress. Without her being close to me, I could not face strangers. I felt so insecure!

## CHAPTER 3

### *The small house*

When I was about nine years old, we moved to a farm close to town. There were two houses on this farm. My dad would be manager for the owner, just as he had been on previous farms. We got the small house close to the main road. My mother was not very happy about this house. We now had only two bedrooms and it was not in a good condition at all. I think what made it all the worse was that the owners borrowed money from my dad to be able to buy this farm.

The other of the two houses was like a fairytale house. It was huge with beautiful gardens, statues and little fountains. It was not an ordinary house. It reminded me of pictures in storybooks. It was totally different from ours, surrounded by trees. It also had a tennis court, which was very unusual in those days.

The owners, Dick and Lorna, came from England, where he had the "Lord" title She was from a lower class than he. We could only guess as to why they left their country, never to go back again. They were wonderful, humble people. Not only did all of us children play together, the parents were also close friends.

There was no need for me to stay with my aunt anymore. I was so happy! From then on, I could sleep in my own bed every night, not just on weekends. We only had a two-minute walk to the main road. From there an old black school bus would be our transport to school.

I remember once it rained so much that the bridge was covered with water—no need to say how happy we all were for this unexpected day without school.

Sometimes the morning mist was so thick that one of the bigger boys would sit on the bus's engine directing the driver where to go! Because of this we would be late for school. I was very scared that this boy, who had thick glasses, could miss the road and we would end up in the field. The thought of being late for school, coming into the classroom and then explaining what happened, caused me a lot of stress.

A few years later Dick and Lorna decided to sell the farm. My dad bought his own farm. He got back the money they borrowed from him. However, they didn't pay him for a whole year's work. Financially this was a huge loss. I don't know why my father didn't stand up for himself.

It was time to say goodbye to the small house. I still remember the day we moved. The house was already empty and everything clean and ready for the next people to move in. In my parent's room there was a little corner shelf against the wall.

I got hold of a small piece of paper. I can't remember the words anymore but I can remember that I wrote a short blessing for whoever may come and stay in that little house again. I carefully put it on the shelf, wondering who will it be, who will receive my little note.

I was 12 when we moved to our own farm, and for three months I had to stay with people in town to be able to go to school. I was hungry all of the time, but I was too shy to ask for more food. In the evenings we had bread and butter for a meal. One thin slice was not enough, but I was too shy to tell them that I was still hungry. And they were not being sensitive to see what was going on. One evening we visited friends of theirs and guess where I was standing during the visit? Behind the passage door, too shy to sit with them. They also lived very far from my school, and I had to walk that distance all by myself. I am so glad that this was only for one school term. I could not wait to escape from this unhappy situation!

After that, wonderful people, who also lived on a farm and had the facility of a school bus, gave my parents the offer that I could stay with them. They were like second parents to me. They gave me so much love and even bought a brand new piano because I needed to practice for my music lessons. Every evening after dinner we all came together in the dining room where we had Bible study. Uncle Danie liked teasing me, not out of meanness, but always saying, "It is because we love you".

# CHAPTER 4

## *Unfulfilled Dreams*

There were many other situations that were very difficult for me. My father, having had a very difficult childhood, had some issues that influenced the lives of his family.

My paternal grandfather was a very harsh man and seldom showed my father any love or affection. Maybe he loved him, but, because of his own bitterness and anger, the easiest thing he had to give to his son was criticism.

We never knew why my grandfather was so very negative and faultfinding, always dominating his family and doing things his own way. My grandmother, for instance, had to wear high-heel shoes, even at home, because he liked it. She had to wear them no matter how bad the pain in her back was. The comfortable shoes my parents gave her were stored away deep inside the closet.

I remember one Christmas Eve we wanted to surprise my grandparents. We went there, singing Christmas carols all the way. When we got there, my grandfather came out of the house. He chased us away, screaming at my dad that he was drunk. I think that was one of the times that hurt my dad the most. All he could do was just stare at my grandfather.

He couldn't believe that what was supposed to be a surprise family gathering would cause him so much pain and false accusation. Without a word he turned back. The joy of spending Christmas Eve with his parents and family was lost. Back home he was very quiet, but we could see tears filling his eyes.

There was another incident, years later after grandfather passed away. My dad, the child who looked after his parents, was not a beneficiary in his will. I still remember the intense pain it caused him. We will never know why he treated my father like that, the good son who cared for his parents—rejected. Many times I could see the love in my dad's eyes for us.

When we were sick he was so concerned and would sit by our beds. He would do anything to fulfill a need, but not once can I remember him saying the words "I love you". He could show it, but he could not say it. He had never heard those words from his father. It is nearly impossible, unless you receive healing, to give away what you've not received. There were no spontaneous actions of little girls running into their dad's arms, sharing their little secrets with him. It is not just the things that happen to us that affect our lives, but also what we didn't receive; the hugs and cuddles...

Many times there was a lack of finances. It would sometimes happen that everything was in place for a good harvest and my dad would make us exciting promises—promises we trusted him for. But then, a sudden hailstorm would end it all in minutes. During those times he would always say to my mom, "It's okay, we as family are still together." There she would stand, as a gentle, faithful woman of God, supporting and encouraging him to keep on going, thanking the Lord that he could see it that way. But for his children it was yet again a broken promise. As adults it is easier to understand, but as children broken promises have lasting effects on our lives. Of course my father didn't mean to do it, it wasn't his fault that a hailstorm destroyed everything.

I remember once I wanted a green pen, not because I needed it; I just really wanted it. I imagined underlining my schoolwork, giving color with this green pen. I liked and pondered the thought of it. It took considerable courage but, the next morning before going to school, I asked my dad if he could give me the money for it. After so many years, I can still remember the disappointment in his eyes because there was no money for it. My little dream was like a bubble, broken in many pieces. It was only a green pen, but for me, as a little girl, it was something special that could not happen. I think it was here that a mindset began in me that you can only ask the Lord for things that you really need. You cannot ask for extra things, or special things, only the necessity.

Our earthly fathers are the first picture of our Heavenly Father we have, and without thinking about it we project what we believe about our earthly fathers onto God the Father. Take a moment and think about your earthly father. Unless your heart has received healing, when you then think about God, you probably have the same feelings. If you are in touch with some of those emotions, start to share with God how you felt; share your heart with Him.

When you are ready forgive your earthly father, repent for where you've judged him and then ask God to reveal to you who He is as your Heavenly Father. If you don't even know your earthly father, or he's been too busy or hiding behind the newspaper, then forgive him for not being there. Unless you received healing, you probably believe that God is not there for you. Maybe your earthly father abused you and caused you much pain. You may be afraid of God the Father … Share your heart. Your Heavenly Father is waiting for you. Let the journey begin!

For many years, if someone would surprise me with a gift that was not for Christmas or my birthday, I, most of the time, gave it away. Not because I did not want it but because it gave me great pleasure seeing someone else enjoying it. It also played into my belief system that special things are not for me.

In Primary School when it was time for lunch break, each child would get a mug of milo with a sandwich and dried or fresh fruit. Although I longed for it myself, I would take the fruit home for my dad, pretending I didn't like it because I knew he would enjoy it. That was more important to me.

I think it was the difficulties of his childhood and his unfulfilled dreams that influenced my dad in many ways. As a young boy, after school and during school holidays, he had to work on the farm.

One time he entered into a competition where he had to write an essay about farming. He won the competition, and the prize was a one year course on farming. It was an all-expenses-paid course at a College of Agriculture. Instead of being proud of his son, my grandfather refused to let him go. That was something my father could never forget—a lost opportunity that could have changed his life. He had many lost dreams.

The responsibility of still providing for his parents as well as his own family, coupled with the pain and frustration of the past could be the reason for the anger that became part of his life. He could be furious in a split second, and fear was added to our lives. In such times we would make sure to stay out of his way.

I remember practicing for my piano lessons while my sisters would keep watch for him as he was coming home. We made sure not to upset him. All of this made me into a child who strove to do everything right. I now know that it was part of why I did not explore and develop risk-taking as a child. It really put who I was in a box. It caused me to be so shy and afraid to do wrong that it had a huge impact on my life.

Despite all of this, we also had wonderful times as a family together. It was very convenient having family that lived close to the ocean and we could visit them quite often. This was a two-way blessing—while we could enjoy wonderful days on the beach, our extended family was looking forward to lots of fresh meat and vegetables from the farm. Usually we would leave just after midnight in our Buick, nicknamed "Old Suzy". Somehow my mom managed to make us a bed on the back seat. "Old Suzy" was big! Mom also made us delicious sandwiches, sausages, snacks and coffee for our journey. More or less halfway, my dad would stop at a picnic spot alongside the road so that we could enjoy all these wonderful foodies. My mother is the virtuous wife as described in Proverbs 31!

At that time there were only gravel roads, and it took us more than twice as long as it would take now to reach our ocean-side destination. We had to go through lots of little towns. I can remember the excitement of waking up when Suzy needed gas. Everybody in this little town except for the people at the gas station were sleeping. There was also a rooster who desperately tried at 3:00 am to wake everybody up! These are memories I will always treasure!

We loved the ocean and had a dad who was now totally different from who he was at home. He was now relaxed and laughed a lot. He bought us lots of bananas and avocadoes which were in abundance at the beach. I could not stop eating bananas!

There was one incident that he could never forget and also something that influenced me 'til this day. Because my sister was a baby at the time, my mom could not go with us to the beach on a certain day. My dad and my aunt took us kids for a swim. At one point

I needed something in the car that was parked close by, but when I walked back I went in the wrong direction for quite some time. At last I realized that I had to turn back, but by that time my dad was totally in shock and running all over searching for me. Until the end of his life he could never forget the joy when seeing, in the distance, a little girl with a red swimsuit coming in his direction. He started running to me, hoping that it was me and not another girl in a red swimsuit.

There were so many emotions going through his mind. When he reached me, it was a mixture of laughing, crying and anger. And for me, I was just too happy to be found and safe again!

# CHAPTER 5

## *The wonder of family*

My sisters were always very special to me. It was important to me to know that they were okay. At one point, three of us were sleeping in one bedroom, each in her own bed. Especially in winter when I would wake up during the night, I was concerned that maybe they were not warm enough, so I would give them some of my blankets. They would wake up the next morning feeling so hot. I was curled up in my bed, missing the blankets that I was so generous to give away during the night! As a little child—always thinking of others who needed something more than I did.

I think my mom had a wonderful time when my youngest sister, nine years younger than me, was born! I decided to do everything for this beautiful little baby. I thought of her as a wonder-child. In my mind, God gave her to us as a special gift. She was so precious to me and I would do anything for her. When it was time for her nap, I would put her in her pram, walking up and down the road 'til eventually she would fall asleep. In my eyes, she was not an ordinary baby.

Besides that, at more-or-less the age of 11, all I wanted to do when I was at home was baking and cooking. My dad especially enjoyed all the dishes, and that inspired me to keep on trying! We lived only seven miles from town, and, usually, on a Saturday morning my parents would go to town, leaving me behind looking after my three sisters. Surely that gave me the opportunity to surprise them with one or another new dish!

I remember one specific day. I cooked them a nice meal, knowing the time they usually got back. But that day they were held up in town for some reason. There was no way that they could contact us. I had so much fear that something bad happened to them. In the meantime I had to keep my nice meal warm in the coal stove, which was not so easy. Every time I heard a car coming down the road, I ran out to see if it was them. At last, when they arrived, it was like a huge burden rolling from my shoulders. It was such a relief!

Once there was a situation that I could not forget. Maybe because I could not understand it. I was about 12 years old when my grandmother and my cousin came to visit. One day the three of us were alone at home. At some point, my grandmother decided to treat us with a snack called "biltong". I loved biltong and was very happy with this announcement. However, my joy did not last for long.

When I saw my grandmother giving my cousin, who was only a year older than me, a much bigger piece, I was very upset. I took it and did not say anything. I was so hurt that I felt like crying. Pretending that I needed the toilet, I went to the outside toilet and got rid of my piece. In my heart I felt that she was more worthy than me. I think my feelings were more intense because it was the same cousin who would not let me play with her dolls. And now she again got the best part of the biltong. Because I loved my grandmother *so much*, the hurt was so much more. During my teenage years, so many times because of illness, my father was also the absent father. Being in hospital, sometimes for months, my mom and her daughters would stay on the farm taking care of everything.

One day while coming from the chicken den with a basket of eggs, my mom thought about the letter she had just received from the doctor telling her that he was fighting for my dad's life in the hospital. Her first reaction was shock and panic. "What are we going to do, how are we going to survive?" But then the Lord brought Psalm 121 to her mind: *"I lift my eyes to the mountains, where does my help come from? My help comes from the Lord, the maker of heaven and earth."* *(NASB)*

From that moment on, she had such peace, knowing that the Lord will take care of us—and He did. Not long after that, my dad came home. He was still very sick but at least he was back home. My mother is an incredible woman of faith. Trusting the Lord in everything is still, this day, a lifestyle for her. She is a testimony for many!

Each day on our way to school, the school bus would pass the hospital where my father was recovering after surgery. In the afternoons, on our way back home, he would stand in the corner of the hospital grounds, waving to us, wiping tears from his eyes. It was so painful for me to see him standing there in his hospital gown. I longed for him to be back home. It was as if there was a huge gap inside of me, a gap that nothing else could fill.

He always had a very special way of celebrating birthdays. When I was young, I did not know the deepness and value of it. Now, after receiving many revelations, I look back and I am amazed at the way he did it. It was not something he did in a hurry. He would stand in front of me, look me in the eyes and thank me for being the daughter I was and for the pleasure I brought them and for everything in my life that he appreciated.

Then he would speak a blessing over me – not a quick-quick blessing but a blessing from deep within his heart. He always did it with tears in his eyes. He did the same to my sisters. Those words of affirmation and blessing did not mean so much for me when I was a child. I don't think that I fully understood it. Looking back now, I realize what he, as a father, really was doing for his children. Those were powerful moments in our lives. Throughout his life he was very sickly. Later, when we were older, he grew close to God and He loved the Lord with all of his heart. His grandchildren only have the best memories of him. He loved them so much, and they always wanted to visit their Oupa Fanie and Ouma Baby (grandparents). One of the ways my mom's love for these little ones was expressed was in sewing and knitting for them. She was, and still is at the age of 95, such a wonderful granny, now knitting for her great grandchildren! Even the ones of them living overseas.

Our maternal grandfather was an amazing, wonderful man of God. He decided to get himself a little house organ, all the way from Canada. Every morning at 4:00 am, he would get up, spending time with the Lord while playing and singing, waking up everyone in the house. He passed away on my sixth birthday. The night before he died, my mom was sitting by his feet, and he said to her: "My daughter, if you will always sit at the feet of Jesus like this, He will take care of you". Now, at her advanced age, my mother still remembers and treasures those words.

On our farm, there was a little dam surrounded by rocks, which was the favorite place to which I would escape when I needed time by myself. It was my way to process all the thoughts that filled my mind. I was the only member of our family who went there regularly. I loved early mornings listening to the birds in the trees, watching them building their nests. I loved experiencing it at the end of the day during the most beautiful sunsets. I found so much peace just sitting there quietly by myself. It became my little dam, and everyone knew where to find me.

It has always been hard for me to say goodbye to wherever I call home. When I was visiting from college, the last thing I did before leaving was to have a few minutes at my little place, praying for my family as I was leaving them behind. I did not like packing my suitcases, and many times my mother would do it for me while I was sitting at my special place. Thank you Mom!

# CHAPTER 6

## *Party time!*

I have wonderful memories of living on the farm. When we were younger, there were a lot of young people in the area, and all were friends. There was much fun to be had, like going to dances in the farmer's hall. There were always a few adults watching over the younger ones. Everyone would dance until midnight, when the party ended. My sisters loved dancing, and so did my parents, but I did not! I had to go because I couldn't stay at home all by myself.

Once there was a huge storm coming, and, because we had to cross a river to reach the dance hall, I wished that it would rain so much that the water would flood the bridge. Then they would have to cancel the party. I was so excited when the rain started pouring and someone called to tell us that no car could cross the bridge because of all the water. Then someone else came with this bright idea—what about a tractor with a trailer? So guess what, that is exactly what happened!

We were transported to the party with a tractor and trailer. And of course, I could not stay at home! Until the age of 14 I had no special friends. During breaks I would be all by myself. I then became friends with a girl in my class. She was a brilliant student and a wonderful friend to me.

I ended my final year of school while I was still 16 years old and during that year I got saved; I gave my life to Jesus. I then became a member of our church.

It was during that time that I wanted to know more about the Lord. I made an appointment with the minister and one day after school I went to see him at his house. I was very nervous, but I knew I had to do it. He explained to me all about salvation and right there in his office I accepted Jesus as my Lord and Savior. I made a lifetime decision to never let go of Him. I was so excited to start this new journey with Him! The scripture the minister gave me for the Confirmation was Isaiah 43:1 *"I have summoned you by name, you are mine"*. This was the beginning of a lifetime journey, and I was very serious about having a relationship with Jesus.

During my final year at school, the older ones sat in the back rows of the school hall. I was watching all of the younger ones in the front rows. I was so concerned about how on earth I could ever love them as the Bible tells me to do. I don't even know them! I thought there would be some kind of special feelings towards them that I did not have. I then decided to write a letter to the minister. His response was to buy myself a Christian book that could explain it to me. I did not do this because we lived on a farm and the only bookshop I knew about in town was the one selling schoolbooks. I had no experience of Christian books except for the Bible.
I did not understand the concept of love as the Ten Commandments says: "Love your neighbor as yourself". For me it was to have a special feeling on the inside. I was very confused.

In school I worked very hard. I loved studying. Together with that, I had to spend many hours practicing for piano exams, therefore I had a schedule for every day of the week, and I was serious about it. The last year of school was no exception. I worked very hard and when the rest of my classmates were looking to the future, making plans, dreaming of the matric farewell (Prom), new dresses and make-up, I was trying to avoid these conversations. For me there was nothing to dream about, nothing to look forward to.

My dad had become very ill and was in a hospital in Johannesburg, hours away from us. My mother had no choice but to be with him. My support system for this important event in my life was not there. I did not have a new dress, or a hairdresser, and I did not want to go. At last my aunt convinced me that I had to go, and gave me one of her dresses to wear. It was a beautiful floral dress—but certainly not the right choice for such a special occasion.

All the girls had hairdresser appointments, giving each other compliments, except for one— me, who had a very kind and helpful aunt who did her best to curl my hair. I was so embarrassed that night. The function was held in the school hall, beautifully decorated. What made everything worse for me was that the highlight of the function was the dance after the meal. That was not fun! I could not wait to go home. On the inside I missed my parents even more because all the other pupils had their parents joining the function.

Without medical aid there were so many bills to be paid, but still my parents' desire—and mine too—was that I should become a teacher. Only a few of us in our class were qualified and chosen to go for it. I don't know how my mother managed it but through her chicken farming she got me the things I needed, while making the most of my clothes herself.

Compared to the other students' wardrobes, I had very little, but for me everything was so special. It was made with love and meant a lot to me.

# CHAPTER 7

## *Farmgirl / Citygirl*

When I first went to college, my parents took me by car. It was not easy for us because from then on, I would mostly only be able to come home during the holidays by train. Luckily, this time my experience by train would be quite different than I had during my first school year!

The car was packed the previous evening. It was still dark when we got up the next morning to start our four-hour drive to Bloemfontein. This was no easy journey for us. For them, their first child was leaving home. For me, it was the beginning of a new season in my life, and I did not know what to expect.

I can still see in my imagination the street with the big trees when we came into the city. I had a mixture of feelings. I feared the moment when it would be time to say goodbye to my parents. Although I prayed about everything, I was still very anxious. When my dad parked in front of the big dormitory of the first-year students, I felt like crying. There were many students with their parents at the college hostel. The different room numbers were all in a container and everyone had to draw a number.

The room I got was a single room. I nearly started to cry. I did not want to be alone in such a new place. They then said that they will make an exception, I can get another chance. The same thing happened again! Miraculously they gave me another chance and this time I had a roommate.

I remember that afternoon looking through the window, crying, as I watched my mom and dad leaving through the College gates. But then, all of a sudden I started to smile! I said to myself, "Don't worry, tomorrow evening you will be on the train, going back home, never to come back to this place again!" The next day however, after connecting with my roommate, I decided to stay, and that was one of the best decisions of my life. I soon realized that the only thing I wanted to do was to be a teacher—I loved working with children.

At the College, the other students soon realized that I was very serious about the Lord. Every Sunday afternoon after lunch I would be part of a group of students going by bus to the poorer areas of the city. I'm truly sad when I look back to those days. We would knock on the door, then after greeting the people, ask them something like: 'If you would die today, do you know where you will go, heaven or hell?' Sometimes they would invite us to come in, but many times doors were slammed in our faces. Not only did we interrupt their privacy, we also interrupted their Sunday afternoon nap and they surely did not like it.

Instead of sharing God's love, we pronounced fear unto them. The fear of spending eternity in hell made them sometimes say the sinners' prayer. I think most of us knew that God loved us, but it was not really a heart revelation of His Love, therefore we could not give His love away in the right manner.

Once a week, a minister from one of the city's churches would come to the hostel. They always held a short sermon after dinner while we were still sitting at the tables.

Among them was a young preacher who was different. It was not because he was young. There was something special in his eyes. Something I desired with all my heart. My explanation for that was that he had a very intimate relationship with the Lord. Out of that place of intimacy, love was flowing through him, touching people around him.

For the practical part of the teacher's course, we had to go to all the different schools in the city. The College provided money for taxis and busses. Many of the students had a much better way of spending the money and decided it would be better to hitchhike and use it as spending money. While other students enjoyed spending money on fun things, I would use it for necessities like clothes, toiletries and even for my train ticket home.

There were many special memories. One of the special moments about being a student was that many times students of the men's hostels would serenade outside of the ladies' hostels, and it would wake us up.

The College was not far from the mid-city, close enough to walk there. I remember one day, a few minutes before closing time of the shops, my friend and I remembered that it was my roommate's birthday the next day and we hadn't gotten her a gift. The only way to get to the shops in time was to hitchhike. Very soon a car stopped. My friend pushed me into the front seat while she got in the back. We then saw that this man was a painter; his clothes had a lot of paint on them. He said "Do you know you cannot open the doors?" He scared us so much when we realized it was true. The doors could not open from the inside! Luckily he was only joking with us; he stopped in front of the shop, jumped out, opened the doors and, with a big smile and a wave of his hand, he went on. Wow! That surely was a relief!

I always booked a taxi to the station when it was time to go home. The days when the College closed for the holiday seasons were always very special. Most of the students had friends or family waiting for them, coming from other places. Only a few of us had to go by train.

My train departed in the late evening. I can never forget the excitement while waiting to hear my name called out that my taxi had arrived. I was too excited to sleep that night, just thinking about seeing my dad waiting for me on the platform. And then, after less than an hour's drive home, I sat at my mom's breakfast table enjoying the special meal she had prepared. These are memories I will always treasure.

# CHAPTER 8

## *Brokenness in school*

When I started teaching, I was part of all of the Christian activities. My first opportunity was at a school in a small town about an hour's drive from home. I loved my job and I loved the children. I realized that there were so many broken children, and if I wanted to make a difference, instead of criticism, I was to give them love—show them that I trusted them and believed in them.

I think my compassion came from my own school days. I can still remember good remarks a teacher gave me. When I was in school I had to make a summary of a book. For some reason mine was a few days late. I expected to be in trouble but afterwards the teachers' remark was: "If you keep on bringing me excellent work like this, you can be late every time. I won't mind." I was so surprised, it made my day! I can still see the exact place in the class where I was sitting, and I can see the teacher as he spoke to me. Today, many years later, I also remember the first sentence of that summary.

Sadly the opposite was also true. No matter what I did, I could never please our Home Economics teacher. She was always picking on me and made me feel no good. I hated going to her class and it was thus no surprise that my final exams in that subject were less than good!

I was the teacher called when a nine or ten-year-old girl tried to end her life because of all the conflict at home. Her parents wanted to divorce, which negatively influenced her schoolwork. Her whole life came to the point that she could not handle it anymore. She thought taking a handful of pills that she found in their house would be the solution. I was just in time to prevent a tragedy, but I had to convince her not to try again. I could only love on this child, giving her hope and telling her how important she was to everybody. Watching this child laughing and playing again was such an inspiration to me. It was clear how words of love and kindness can bring a turnaround in a child's life.

Sadly the opposite is also true. So many people carry hurt and pain caused by negative words spoken to them by teachers. But we can forgive these people and in the Name of Jesus break the words that they have spoken over our lives and ask Jesus what *He* says about us. In the end that is what really matters, and that is where we receive freedom from these situations. He wants us to share with Him all that happened to us, allow the emotions to flow and give it to Him. He truly cares.

Then there was the 12-year-old boy who was not doing well at school anymore. All the teachers were battling with him, telling him how disappointed they were with him. Although he was not in my class, I decided to give him some help after school. The only thing I did was to motivate him, together with love, and to show him that I trust him and that I know that he is an amazing boy. That totally changed that boy's life, as well as his schoolwork.

Financially, my parents were still going through a hard time. There were so many medical bills to be paid. Sometimes I would put some money in their wallets without letting them know about it. It was not much, because I had not much. But I knew that my little gift would somehow help them.

I remember once I got a lift from another teacher to a town close to where my parents lived. I had to spend that weekend with my aunt who lived in that town. There was no money for gas to come and fetch me to spend the weekend with my family. Although I understood the situation, my heart longed to go home for the weekend.

During my first years of teaching I met an Engineering student. He was a good guy and very soon he was very serious about our relationship, in such a way that he wanted me to marry him. At the age of 19 I surely was not ready for marriage. But a few years later my younger sister got married at the same age. I felt that people started looking at me with a mixture of compassion and curiosity on their faces while asking funny questions like, "When is it your turn?" or "You know she is your younger sister!" And then, as if they were looking through me, "don't worry, the right man will come, just make sure you have enough trousseau." In the meantime they didn't know my trousseau kist was already packed with linen, towels and nice goodies...all bought from the travelling salesmen who knew what product the young teachers were looking for.

I was starting to wonder about this. Maybe they were right. What if there was something wrong with me? There came a point when I decided to go for the guy who overloaded me with gifts and flowers. Every month on our engagement day a huge bunch of flowers were delivered in my classroom and everybody said, "Wow!" And I thought to myself—I'm not in love with him but surely he will be a good husband to me. I also felt sorry for him because of his bad relationship with his family. Little did I know what was coming!

During those days I was very serious about the Lord. I read my Bible, had devotions twice a day, but I cannot remember asking Him about marrying this man. I was still praying to a God somewhere in the distance, not expecting any answers. It really was more like religion; it was one sided. I did not have a relationship with God.

Maybe I did not ask because of that lack of relationship, I really can't remember. This decision caused me so much pain in my life. If it was not for my precious daughters I don't know if I would ever have survived that marriage.

A day after our wedding this loving man, in one moment, became a total stranger to me. My wedding day was a bright summer day in December. Everything was perfect—I had a beautiful dress, the ceremony, the reception afterwards. But in my heart there was a mixture of feelings. I knew that the love I had for this man was not the real thing, but in a sense I was happy. I bluffed myself with things like "he is serious about the Lord, he reads his Bible, he will be a good husband". But deep inside I was not convinced about it. In the next few weeks I would realize that he did all these things only to impress me.

There was something else that caused much stirring inside of me. The week after our wedding, my mother would go to the same city at the coast where we planned to spend our honeymoon. She needed a huge kidney operation. She was very ill and that was not easy for me. On the outside I had this big smile, but on the inside it was a total different situation.

# CHAPTER 9

## *Step without faith*

The day after the wedding, while on our way to our honeymoon accommodation, I asked if I could drive for a while—actually it was my car! Those few words triggered something in him. In a moment this loving man totally changed. Not once was he angry with me in the past, and now he was furious! I was so confused, I did not know how to handle the situation. A few days after our wedding was my 26th birthday.

On that day, my grandfather suddenly passed away. I was on my honeymoon, supposed to be happy. With my mother in hospital, my grandfather having suddenly passed away and my husband totally different than just days before, I was not happy at all. I was so stressed. There was no sign anymore of the loving person I agreed to marry.

I had a beautiful engagement ring. My wedding ring had seven diamonds. So many times in future, with tears in my eyes, I would look at those diamonds, calling them diamonds of tears.

On our way back home, I was dreaming. But this time, I was dreaming of how to divorce my new husband. He had another surprise waiting for me. He had psychological problems which resulted in his not wanting to share me with anybody, including my parents. He was jealous and at times spiteful when I wanted to visit them. Before the marriage it had been just the opposite. My new neighbors wanted to meet me, but as soon as we became friends he would tell me how bad they were. He was a farmer without formal training. In his eyes the educated, particularly teachers, were common. They were nothing! (like me!)

He always had pain, although doctors could not find anything wrong with him. He went from one doctor to another, experiencing all sorts of medicine.

When I was three months pregnant with Marguerite, our doctor did not know what to do for him anymore, and he sent him to a specialist in another town. This doctor was a few hours away. He decided to perform an operation and see if he could find something wrong. This was the beginning of a three month period in hospital. As for me, it was three months of living in a little Volkswagen car in the parking area of the hospital, making use of the hospital's facilities.

Looking back, I don't know how I survived while pregnant, eating junk food all the time and living in a small car. I could not sleep, while he was comfortable in his hospital bed, demanding that I be at his side all of the time. I was very concerned about him. I was not able to stand up for myself. The day before he went home, I went to the grocery store, and an elderly woman, a total stranger, came to me and started

talking to me. When she heard about my situation she asked me to come and stay with her and her husband. So nice, but of course I had to decline.

After the surgery, the doctor could not understand why the pain was still so severe. In the meantime, the patient was starting to get addicted to very strong painkillers. Back home, he went to see two doctors in different towns, getting prescriptions for this medicine from both of them. They did not know about each other until I told them and they immediately stopped prescribing. Then he overdosed himself with painkillers that he could buy over the counter.

Sometimes he had so much "pain", and since we lived close to town, the doctor would come and give him an injection. In minutes the pain would be gone—he never knew that this was not a painkiller, only vitamins.

Once he had shock treatments that had such a negative effect on him that he nearly killed me. I could see the hatred and fury in his eyes. He had his hands around my neck. He was out of his mind. But at that moment my father-in-law came in from nowhere and he let me go.

I once asked the neighbors to visit us. When it was time to leave, they would pretend that their car was broken. I planned this with them just so they could spend the night with us because I was too scared for myself and the children to be alone with my husband. My daughter Marguerite was just three years old. I gave them all our guns in case he decided to shoot us, as he had promised many times that he would.

The doctor instructed him not to take any alcohol. But several times, when we were at a function he'd ignore the doctor and take alcohol together with strong painkillers. It was just too much, and he would pass out for the rest of the night and not be able to take his family back home. Somebody else would then drive him home with our car, while friends would take me and my children back home. I was so embarrassed and the little respect that I still had towards him was running out very quickly. At some point trust was broken permanently.

I knew he loved our three daughters, but he never showed them any compassion or love. He was so involved in his "sickness" that he did not care about his family. He provided for us and for him, it was the way it had to be done. If he could provide a house, food on the table and things we needed, he would count for a good father and husband.

He was in no way interested in helping me with the children. I also could not trust him. Once we came back from a visit to my parents. While unloading the car, I suddenly saw Marguerite, about three years old, sitting on the kitchen floor with his pistol in her hand.

It shocked me to the core! His carelessness about something dangerous like a pistol deeply concerned me—more even because he chose a diaper bag to store the pistol.

As a farmer, you are your own boss and you can be at home as often as you like to be. He enjoyed that privilege and used the opportunity to be on his bed and was in no way interested in spending time with his family.

During this time I was offered a teacher's position at the school. But because he and my father-in-law did not like the idea, I had to refuse an opportunity where I could escape, in some way, from my situation at home.

While pregnant with my second child, Lisl, I had problems that nearly caused a miscarriage and therefore the doctor instructed me to stay home and rest as much as possible.

During this time, one Saturday afternoon, my father-in-law suddenly passed away while in the field, having had a heart attack. He had three children, my husband and two daughters, and he owned three farms. Usually each child would inherit a farm but in this case the one daughter got two farms while my husband merely had the use of "his" farm. He could farm it but it didn't belong to him.

I could understand that. Because of all of his hospital experiences and high medical bills, his dad was concerned about leaving him with the responsibility of such a big farm, owned for many years by their family. What I could not understand was that he was in no way concerned about myself children and the children.

With nobody to check on him anymore, he went mad, buying

new implements, wasting money, so that in the end he had to quit farming and get himself a job in town. So we moved. Luckily he could still buy us a brand-new house. We did not know that this would only be my children's and my home for just a few years.

# CHAPTER 10

## *My daughters, my treasures*

A few months after my father-in-law's sudden death, Lisl was born on the same day that Marguerite was born but five years apart. My husband was very proud when telling everybody about his daughters, but that is where it all ended. When Lisl was close to a year he, one day, decided to pick her up. She refused and he was very shocked. She was just a baby, but because of his lack of interest in the children, she didn't really know him. He blamed me for that.

I was the only one going to church. I enjoyed going just to escape from a depressed, unhappy situation, if only for a few hours. I will always remember the day when Marguerite decided she needed to make change while giving something for the offering! She put something in the offering plate and then took some change. That caused some laughing and giggling around us!

When Landi was born, about four years later, our relationship was so bad that as I was going into labor, I waited until he left for work that morning, then I went to the hospital on my own. I was too embarrassed to go with him, so I took the car and drove to the hospital, parking at the back where nobody could see the car. I was very nervous while going to the office, telling them I'm not sure if I need to be there, will they please check, just maybe, I need to be there?? Needless to say, a few hours later my little girl was born! She was born with a head full of beautiful brown curls.

I then started a course in writing—something I had always wanted to do. I enjoyed every moment of it, and after a while a few of my children's stories were published in a magazine. I then took a course in short stories, and all the work that I sent in came back with very good results, motivating me to go for it. At last the stress at home with a 24-hour a day depressed husband became too much and I gave it up, leaving me with an emptiness of what could have been.

All of this made me into a broken person with so much pain on the inside (but a smile on the outside). I hoped that my parents would not see what I was going through. My life was falling apart. There was a bridge on the main road, and I started visualizing how I would take the car, drive into it, making sure it will be the end of me. However, the thought of leaving my precious children behind kept me from going through with it.

Once a year we would go to the beach for one week. As soon as we were booked into our accommodation, usually an apartment close to the beach, my husband would go in his own direction. He only came back at night time and was totally separated from his family. He simply did not care about us. Many times he would eat steak in a restaurant, and we would eat something simple in the apartment, as there was no money for all of us to eat out. He didn't care.

When I talked with my pastor about everything, he told me that my case was special because of his psychological problems. This was far too big for me to solve with marriage encounter books. Like my dad, my husband also had no good memories of his childhood. At the age of more-or-less seven years, his parents divorced and he was, in a very strange way, taken away from a wonderful Christian mother to stay with a critical, angry father and a stepmother who did not care about him. He did not receive love, so he did not know how to give it away. To get attention, he had to do something, and for him, pain was the solution. He was a very broken man.

When Landi was a baby, she could be totally fine and then all of a sudden she could have an extremely high fever. When she was about one year old, the doctor sent her for X-rays. I was so worried about my baby and so tired of the disappointments of my marriage that I somehow, unbelievably, did not hear or did not take in all of what the doctor said that day. All I knew was that we had to go to Pretoria, a few hours away, for more tests.

After we came home, our doctor suggested that I take the children to the beach for a short vacation. Landi would be fine because of medicine they gave her, and as he said I urgently needed a break too. He knew about my situation and already had given up on my husband, who just had another surgery. Instead of staying home, my husband decided to go with us. For me it only meant more stress. He could be helpful in no way.

The second day, Landi began to have a fever, and I immediately called my doctor. I can still remember his words—"wait 'til late afternoon when its cooler (our car didn't have airconditioning), and then drive during the night, as quick as you can to Pretoria"—six to seven hours away.

I was so scared, I called my parents and I remember saying to my mom, "I don't want to lose my child!!" They were praying, and I started driving. I didn't know the city, and before I got onto the highway I nearly caused an accident. But at last we were on our way.

I switched on the emergency lights and I drove at a high speed, not thinking clearly, just praying and at the same time panicking. At one point I was pulled over by the police, but one look of the officer into the car and he said, "Go! Just be careful".

Behind me was a little girl with a fever that would not let her go and next to me a husband who was not able to give me any support.

Halfway there, we stopped at my sister's house and she immediately took Landi and me to their hospital, where she was kept in an ice tent 'til 4:00 am. I was with her all the time. We then had to leave for Pretoria where the urologist was expecting us.

The doctor's instruction was to give her the medicine for fever in two hours. I went to pick up the rest of my family, but before we could leave, her temperature was extremely high again and I had to give her more medicine. I was now used to driving at a high speed but I was so, so tired!

# CHAPTER 11

## *The God of miracles!*

Arriving in Pretoria, I had a hard time finding our way. I did not know that city either, but at last I found the hospital. Luckily we had family there and they could take care of my children and husband while I was at the hospital with Landi.

At the hospital I gave the urologist her X-rays, he looked at it and said to me—"your child only has one kidney, but don't worry, we are here to help you". Then it struck me—that was what they said when they took the X-rays. "Your child only has one kidney." How is it possible that I could miss it??

In the meantime my parents and family, without knowing what the doctor said, started calling people, asking them to pray for Landi. They had to pray for her fever and the cause of it; that is all they knew. In the early morning hours, one lady was woken up by the Lord, hearing the words "pray for a kidney". She did not know why, as she didn't know about the x-rays. But she started praying for a kidney.

We also knew about a medical doctor who prays for people and many miracles happen, so somebody called him also to pray. That night I stayed with Landi again. Early the next morning they took X-rays for a second time. I had an appointment with the urologist later that morning.
When I came in there, he had two sets of X-rays in his hands. "I can't explain it", he said, "It's a miracle! Your child had one kidney and now she has two!" As for me, I could not stop thanking the Lord for giving my precious little girl back to me! He is so amazing, so wonderful! Thank you Lord! That was a creative miracle!!

Back home, I started seeing people like the minister, the doctor, a lawyer and also a marriage counsellor who was in another town. When I went into the counsellor's office, I asked her if she doesn't get depressed when hearing so many sad stories. Her reply with a big smile was, "No, you get used to it and learn not to be emotionally involved." After hearing my story, she looked at me with tears in her eyes—"What I need to say to you is not easy. You need to end this marriage as soon as possible. If not, you will, in coming years, blame yourself and it will be a double blame because your children may become like their father."

Walking out, on my way back home, I had such a relief, but there was another side of it. How will I be able to do that? I did not say anything to my husband because I did not want to hurt him by taking his children away from him. So I kept quiet, praying for an outcome. A little while later, without me knowing it, he went to see the social worker. I was amazed when *he* told me that she wants to see me.

She was very kind, but I did not know what to expect because he was there first to meet with her. I admit I was surprised when she said to me "I give you two weeks to make a decision; this marriage can't work." But still I felt sorry for him, not realizing he was seeing another woman. Out of the blue, he asked if I would start the divorce.

Things were now very tense and I decided it was better for my children and me to move out. He did not care what happened to us, he did not even know where we were going to stay. Through friends, people we didn't even know offered their "rondavel" (a thatch-roof cottage) in their backyard, totally opposite of our beautiful new house. He gave us the second car, which was a red Volkswagen Beetle, surely not in a condition to be our only car.

Only a few people really knew what I was going through and

that we were getting a divorce. I was always smiling, pretending everything was fine. I now realize it was not good going through all the trauma by myself, that it could have been a time of friends praying for me, supporting me. It was so hard!

Because I was the one who started the divorce, I had to go to court in Bloemfontein, a few hours away. I had the support of my lawyer who took me there. I was so nervous when we approached this magnificent building.

There were a few other people also waiting for the same reason. I felt so cheap and miserable. Because the two advocates involved on either side had already come to an agreement, this would only be a formality taking a few minutes. I will always remember the relief when I walked out of that building! The nightmare was finally over!

The day after the court case, my three children were already in bed, and while looking at their beautiful sleeping faces, the reality of being divorced struck me for the first time. How and where will I raise them as a single parent? At that moment the Lord so clearly spoke to me: "*Even to your old age and grey hairs I am He. I am He who will sustain you (and your children)*" Isaiah 46:4.

Until this day, I hold onto this as a Promise of the Lord. Every time there is a situation where fear is involved, I would remind myself of this Promise.

I knew we could not stay in the same town with my ex-husband and the new woman in his life. I felt it was not fair towards my children, and therefore we packed and moved to a small town, close to my parents, a few hours away. We rented a small house close to the school, and we all slept in one room, although there were two bedrooms. My mom and dad bought us furniture for the home and school uniforms for the children.

I immediately made an appointment with the headmaster at the school. He had so much sympathy in his eyes when he looked at us, saying something like "How is it possible that a man can leave a family like this?"

# CHAPTER 12

## *The one horse town*

Within a few months I was able to start teaching again. It was a sad day when the headmaster got promotion after just a year and moved to the city. He was a good man who cared for people and his students, and I would miss him.

According to the court, my ex-husband was only allowed to see the children when I was present. He could not take them anywhere on his own. During his first visit, a few minutes after he arrived, Marguerite took her bicycle, pretending she wanted something from the shop, only two minutes away. She came back just before he left that afternoon. Our neighbors, an eldery couple, checked on her to see that she was safe. She stayed in the shop for hours.

With his second visit, his girlfriend came with him, and my children could only stare at them, sitting close to each other on the couch, holding hands. It was a great relief when they left early that afternoon. Marguerite, at 11, was old enough to realize why there was a divorce.

Landi at the age of two was still too small. Lisl, six, was the one who kept asking about her dad. That day when they left she said to me—"There is no need for him having this girlfriend." From that day on, she did not ask about him anymore.

Our life in our new town was simple. We bought ourselves a collie dog. On weekends we would pack our little red Volkswagen, take our Collie and go to my parents about 45 minutes away. Before we could leave town, we first had to stop at the gas station but not for gas. Our little Volkswagen could not get enough oil. He absorbed a few tins a week! Luckily this went on only for a few weeks when my brother-in-law gave us a very special deal on one of his cars. With our Peugeot we could drive in style.

I enjoyed my role as a kindergarten teacher and had the privilege to have Lisl as well as Landi in my class. This was the "one horse town where the horse had died" that Marguerite now speaks about when she recounts her early life.

When my children were sick, the first thing we would do was to pray. We had a good relationship with the elderly couple who lived in the house next to us; they were always concerned about us. There were people in this small town that were kind to us, but sadly the opposite was also true.

There were some who really looked down on us, seeing us as the poor family who came to live amongst them. Marguerite was very aware of this. As soon as I started teaching, the attitude of some people toward us changed.

After a few years, I met a man and I married again, not realizing this man had similar problems as my first husband, and some extras. Today, I can't believe that I could not see what was going on. I was desperate to give my children somebody who could be a real father to them. My heart was not healed from my first experience as well as the deeper roots of lies about myself that had made me feel okay to marry my first husband. The lies we believe about ourselves, about life and others, are like blinders in life. Jesus came that we may know the Truth and the Truth will set us free.

For me this was even a worse situation, because now there were five daughters involved. He had brought two more daughters into the marriage. It seemed his children could do nothing wrong; mine could do nothing right. We stayed less than an hour from my parents, and if I wanted to visit them for a Sunday lunch, he first would ask his daughters how they felt about it. Usually they agreed, but one time, the most important one time for me and my children, he and his two daughters did not want to go, and we all stayed home.

That one special time was the last chance I had to see my dad alive. The next Wednesday morning he unexpectedly passed away. All my sisters with their children were on the farm and so spent time with him during his last days...but not me and my three daughters.

It was a Wednesday morning, a week before he would turn 73. He didn't feel well that morning. My mother quickly went to feed her chickens. Walking back she was thinking about his birthday, what she would prepare. They never invited people, the neighbors always just came to celebrate his birthdays, knowing that my mother had a wonderful meal ready for them. Coming into their bedroom, she was just in time to see him pass away.

My sister who was with them called the ambulance and she then called me. The children were all in school and my husband was working in the fields. I remember grabbing Landi and driving at high speed to the farm.

I arrived minutes before the ambulance. When I walked into the room I had the feeling that he was still there, lying on the bed, waiting for me to come. At that moment shock, guilt and sorrow all together went through my mind. With tears flooding I kissed him on his forehead, saying farewell. Everything was so unexpected and unreal, I could not think clearly. Reality would hit us later.

The day of the funeral we were allowed to look at him once more. After everybody left I was still standing there, staring at him, not wanting to let go of him. About then I so clearly heard the words "I will never leave him or forsake him ". Then I felt free to go.

This time was not easy for me. The thing that made it even worse was that I had the opportunity to spend time with him, and I was not there.

I felt so angry with myself for not going on my own that previous Sunday. For a very long time, I had a guilt feeling about it. It was an eye-opener. I then knew this marriage was going the wrong direction.

At last I made an appointment with a psychologist in the neighboring town. After a few appointments, some with the children along, it was no surprise when he too advised me to end the marriage because it could not work. We were like two separate families under one roof. I had to pay all my children's expenses, even their part of the groceries, the mortgage payment (on his house), electricity, etc. If they were with us when we went somewhere, I had to help pay for gas as well. Once we came back from vacation and on our way back we stopped for lunch.

The waiter thought it was one bill but my husband would not even wait to do the calculations later. It had to be done now! And there, in this busy lunch hour, in front of many people, we had to separate the bills. From that day on I paid my part together with my children's. He paid for himself and his children separately.

I cannot describe all the pain and guilt I went through during those few years. Marguerite, my oldest, tried to avoid the situation at home by being involved with many school activities and visiting her friends whenever possible. She spent many weekends at the minister's house or with friends of ours who lived on a farm. She and their daughter were in the same class. I remember once I was standing outside, so angry with myself, even hating myself for bringing my children into this situation. Lisl tried to handle the situation by reading books in her room, which she shared with Landi. She did not talk much. One day I was sick in bed, and when I looked up, this little girl was standing in the door, just staring at me. I could see worry and also sadness in her eyes. She did not say a word. I was so touched by that. Guilt was building up inside of me—like a builder placing bricks of guilt, one by one on top of each other.

I thought that Landi, my youngest, was handling it the best. What I did not realize was that deep inside she had a great deal of pain. Pain that would last until adulthood.

# CHAPTER 13

## *A letter and a dream*

After her final school year, Marguerite decided to take a course at the college in Pretoria. She couldn't wait to go, starting a new season in her life. It was only a three hour drive, but we decided to stay over that night. I was surprised to see how small her bedroom was, and I will never forget her words "You could be very lonely in a room like this." It so touched my heart, it felt like an extra load on me. But, in a day or two, everything changed and even more when she was chosen as the "first year student" of the hostel.

One day I decided to give her room back home a proper cleaning while she was not there. While doing that, I saw a piece of paper on the bookshelf. I made a decision in my life to never read what does not belong to me. For me it was like stealing with your eyes. But, that day, I just knew I had to check on that piece of paper.

It was a letter written by Marguerite and the content broke my heart. She was telling a friend of the emotional pain she was going through because of this marriage. I was standing there with the letter in my hand, knowing there had to be a solution for this unhappy situation! At that moment I knew it was time again to make a decision. But I could not imagine going through a divorce and all those emotions again.

My husband could get angry very easily and then ignore my children and me for days. It would happen sometimes that he was too angry to sleep. Around midnight he would pull me out of the bed, trying to convince me how bad I treated him. He threatened to take an overdose of medication, or to drive into the dark not to come back again. At first I tried to stop him.

After a few times I did not care anymore. One day, during an argument, he said that he didn't care about me anymore. Words that he later would regret many times.

That night I had a dream. In the dream a very poisonous snake tried to bite me. I asked my husband for help but he refused and the snake bit me. When I told him about the dream, his response was: "Maybe I am the snake!" And I was thinking: "maybe you are right!" That evening I moved out of our bedroom never to go back again.

Divorce is never easy, even if you are the one walking out. To go through a second divorce in the span of just a few years was difficult for the children as well. This time I made a vow never to marry again. I blamed myself for bringing my children into this situation. Years later, during ministry sessions I was set free from that vow, because I did not want my daughters to be influenced by my negative attitude. I wanted them to have healthy relationships. Besides, in my Bible there are three pieces of paper with their names on it. On these little papers I also declare a blessing over them and their marriages and their children.

My mother moved and now was staying a few houses from us. She had a two bedroom apartment, separate from her house, where I could go with Lisl and Landi. Without my mother things would have been even worse. She was always there for us, encouraging me to keep going, no matter what. Coming home after a day at school, she always had a meal ready for us.

I was still teaching at the school and because a music teacher decided to leave, I was moved from kindergarten to the music department. I was not fully qualified for that position, but I decided to make it work and with the support of the music inspector I got a very good report. The teacher who left then, all of a sudden, decided she wanted her job back. The Principal for some reason decided to make things difficult for me, expecting me to do things he knew I could not do, so that I decided to leave. I had no choice.

I then got a Kindergarten position in another town, but this was only for three days a week. They asked me to work five days, having more classes to teach than anyone else—but only being paid for three days. Because there was no other option, I did it. After two years my position was down to only two days a week. I heard about a position at a school in Qua-Qua for three days a week. It was an hour away from where we stayed and in a different direction from the first school. I was very excited to get the job, although it was only for a few months.

In a certain way, this new job was a huge challenge. Together with a few other teachers, we would leave in minibuses in the early morning and come back late in the afternoon. This was a very high risk area with lots of criminals. Every day we took a different route up to the school trying to avoid any attacks. The other teachers taught me how to do cross-stitching, and that was what we all did while on our way back home every day. We cross-stitched our way through the gauntlet.

# CHAPTER 14

## *The new South Africa*

Everything happened at the same time. When my job was over in Qua-Qua, it was time for the most important election in South Africa. It was an election that would bring big changes in every way. In the new South Africa, where before there were two official languages, there now were 11. The four provinces were divided into nine. And most importantly every person 18 years and older could vote, regardless of race. We had our first black president.

Job situations changed drastically; many people lost their jobs and were replaced. Because I did not have a full time position, I was one of them. A friend spoke to a real estate agency in Pretoria, and they asked me to come for an interview. Very soon Lisl, Landi and I were on our way to Pretoria. I was excited, but I never could have known what this new season in our lives would mean.

My job changed from teacher to real estate agent. As soon as I got training and understood the business, I started enjoying it and making things happen. I was on a roll, and very soon they asked me to share with their successful agents how I did it. They could not believe that this quiet woman from a small town could be successful in this totally different job situation. However, it was very hard work. I worked seven days a week from early morning into late evening. It was not easy. I was sometimes so tired, physically as well as emotionally. Only the Lord could get me through this. I never wanted to live in a city, but now here I was, having had no choice. I was depending on maps to go from point A to point B. It was hard work but I knew I had to make this work.

The agency put so much pressure on the employees. You had to, as they said, eat and sleep property if you wanted to be successful. There was no focusing on anything else. I once signed a contract at midnight. What made things even worse was that we had only one car between the four of us. Everyone was going in different directions. At one point Lisl was waitressing in mid-city in the evenings. I had to set the alarm for 2:00 am so I could be ready to pick her up some time between 3:00 and 4:00 am. I would sleep on top of the blankets, fully dressed, so that I could quickly get up and go.

One Sunday afternoon coming home after having to show a house, I was totally stressed and tired. When Marguerite saw me, her reaction was—"Mom, you bring a negative attitude into the house." I was shocked but I knew it was the truth and I had to do something about it. But I could not see how. I had to work, work, work no matter what.

A day came that I was invited to a meeting for an opportunity for international network marketing. I immediately felt to join and was so fascinated and excited and very soon became one of the leaders, receiving a cheque from overseas every month. Then the government decided to do an investigation on this business, which took a few months. Many of our team decided to quit. Although there was nothing wrong with the network, it was totally legal, too much harm had already been done. People lost trust in the business after hearing of an investigation. After that, I was invited many times to different Network marketing opportunities but somehow it never worked out; it was as if the doors were just closed.

I always told my family about these opportunities. In the beginning they were interested but later on they saw it as schemes and would not even listen anymore. So I kept it to myself. The reason I had gotten involved was that I was so desperately in need of extra income. I tried almost everything possible to meet our needs.

For a long time I only had one pair of shoes, I was able to make my own clothes and because of my size, many times as some of my family members outgrew their clothes, they would pass them on to me. I was always very thankful for that, but at the same time I trusted that the day would come that I would be able to buy the clothes of my choice once more.

I went to church, and organized a cell group at our apartment once a week. I made an effort to meet with other Christians and desired the peace I could see in their eyes. I desperately tried to have more intimacy with the Lord, but He, many times, felt so far away.

I had to be at the office in the early morning, while Landi's school was in the opposite direction, and she required transport. I had to schedule my appointments in such a way so that I could be in time to pick her up after school. In the midst of this, Marguerite and Lisl also needed transport. It brought a great deal of relief the day Marguerite got her own car, a brand-new Uno! One night after we had our home group we all retired to the parking area, praying over her little car.

Once, when I had the most 'sold' signs in the area that I worked in, one of the country's largest agencies asked me to join them, partnering with one of their agents. I was not sure what to do. I prayed about it but did not really believe for direction. So I decided to go for it because of what others said. It was an honor to be part of such a group.

What I did not realize was that my new partner's sales were at the bottom of the ladder. After working together for a few weeks, we were second from the top. She was very excited, walking around telling everybody about ' her" sales. She received all the compliments, not mentioning my name at all.

She was a very classy woman. People talked about how well-dressed she was, while wondering what she would wear the next day. But for me, most of my clothes were made by my mother. It was such a contrast. I, many times, wondered what she was thinking when she looked at me wearing the same shoes every day. She had a big selection, with all the different outfits she owned. It did not bother me though, because the only thing that was important to me was to give my children the things they needed.

She would often talk about having a lady working for her at home and what she was cooking for dinner. They had roast beef, potatoes, vegetables, etc. I didn't say anything to her but I knew that my children and I would be eating sandwiches.

She was not only beautiful and modern, she was also very clever. Although I've signed many contracts on my own while with this one and other agencies, she scared me enough about what would happen if I would make a mistake on a contract that I started letting her do much of the paper work. She preferred to take care of that. I was used to working hard, being out in the community, and I enjoyed being with clients.

Very soon she was staying in the office, pretending she needed to be there in case someone would call. I would then bring in a buyer, and she would fill in the contract, then take it to the manager, pretending it was her sale.

Her attitude towards me changed dramatically. She wasn't the kind partner that I started with anymore. I felt it impossible to work with her any longer and I decided to go back to the previous agency where I did not have to share my commission with somebody else. As I look back, my self-worth was so low, I did all the work and allowed my partner to take all the credit.

If one could work in the upmarket areas, big commissions could be earned, but in the middle class areas there was much less to be earned. The agency took half of it, and on top of that there are taxes to be deducted. There could also be another amount deducted if I'd sold a house that was listed by another agent in my same agency.

I now know that when we do not know who we are, others will take advantage of us, and we may not even realize it. During that time I was not in a community of believers that could speak into my life. I needed people around me with whom I could share my heart; sometimes others can see in our lives what we cannot see.

# CHAPTER 15

## *Making ends meet*

Financially it was not easy. In some way, each of my daughters were still depending on me. Working only for commission was not the easiest way to do it. Sometimes it was as if there was a battle in my mind. The Bible, I knew, gives us all these promises of provision, why then was it not true for me? I would memorize scripture, speak it out loud over and over, but nothing changed, except that my stress would increase. I could physically feel my eyes constrict. It was like the words went up in the air and vanished.

I did not understand that they were not words spoken out of trust and relationship to a listening Heavenly Father—a Father who so loves His children and only wants the best for them. It was just words, and that was what was making the difference between real communication with my Father and sounds bouncing off the ceiling. We can know the truth intellectually, but it only impacts our lives when it becomes heart revelation.

The way we grow up affects how we see life, and, of course, it is different for each person. The financial disappointments I had growing up as a child had a deep impact on my thinking. I'm not blaming my parents, those were hard years and it was my father's heart's desire to give us all we needed. As an adult I can understand about the green pen, but for Sarah, as a child, it was a big disappointment. The promises that could not be realized after hail destroyed the harvest also had a deep impact. Without really thinking about it, I think we develop negative expectations, and the lies we believe hinder us from breaking into what the Lord has for us. It is important to know that when we look deeper at our lives we are not dishonoring our parents or blaming them. We are simply looking deeper for our own healing and freedom—for the renewing of our minds, as Paul said in Romans 12:2.

What can make things even worse is that the Word is very clear about what we say is exactly what we get. James 1:8 states it very clearly – *"But when you ask you must believe and not doubt because the one who doubts is like a wave of the sea blown and tossed by the wind. That person should not expect to receive anything from the Lord. Such a person is doubleminded and unstable in all they do."* (New International version).

Surely, despite the fact that I was speaking scripture all the time, I was a double-minded person, unable to receive what my Heavenly Father so desired to give me.

In the Kingdom of God, it is about our hearts first. God loves the wealthy and He loves the poor. Some of the poorest places have some of the wealthiest people in spirit. Places where they've seen God multiply their food, they've seen God heal, those people know His heart. And some of the wealthiest people are the poorest in spirit, where they depend on themselves, not knowing there is so much more in Him. His plans for us are always bigger than what we can see ourselves, and we can only know those plans as we know His Heart. God wants all people wealthy and poor to know Him, to know His heart for who He really is, and to be walking in all He has for each one of us. Each one's path is unique.

Earthly wealth's impact is temporary unless it is Kingdom minded and legacy focused, making a difference in the world, not as good works but fueled by our love for our King, advancing His Kingdom. This world is temporary, as my mother has said many times "there is no underground spending", meaning you cannot take it with you, but it can impact the world now.

I'm so grateful for every person, friends and family, who were able to financially help me in times of need that they were aware of. Many times I just kept my situation to myself. At the time I felt so ashamed, but now I know that when they gave to this someone in need, it was as if they give to Jesus Himself. He blesses every person who has poured into my life. It has been a journey of breaking free from false beliefs, ungodly expectations, poverty mentality and bad decisions that I made in my life. How amazing is the Grace of Jesus Christ. This is the message of the Cross: divine exchange.

I was so stressed making ends meet that most of the time I did not tithe. When I did, I would first pay the rent, electricity etc. and give some amount of what was left. I did not realize that this would be an open door for the enemy to steal from me. At last, after years, I realized I could do far more with 90% blessed by the Lord than 100% without His blessing. He doesn't need my money, but trusting Him with my tithe shows where my heart is. Do I really trust Him?

He is after my heart. Is my trust in Him or in myself?
Mal. 3: 8-10 states it very clearly. *"Will a man rob God? Yet you rob Me. But you ask. How do we rob You? In tithes and offerings. You are under a curse – the whole nation of you – because you are robbing Me. Bring the whole tithe into the storehouse, that there may be food in My house. Test Me in this, says the Lord Almighty and see if I will not throw open the floodgates of heaven and pour out so much blessing that you will not have room enough for it."* (New International version). It is the only place in the Bible where the Lord says "test Me in this".

Many times it happened that I only had 20 cents for the offering. When the basket came to me, I would quickly put my hand in and out hoping nobody saw my tiny amount. Every time, the Holy Spirit would remind me about the poor widow and her offering, and that He is looking at the heart, not the amount.

Especially during the years of doing Real Estate, I did not

understand the power of the mind. I made one huge mistake. I always said, "If only I could get enough commission to pay bills like rent etc., I will be glad". That is exactly what would happen, though many times there was not even enough to pay those bills.

There were months with no sales, but there were also months with several sales. Nevertheless it was always difficult. Many times I would wake up during the night. During those hours the problems seemed so much bigger. There were many hours that I could not sleep. I was physically and emotionally totally burned out. At one point the office was located in a little shopping center and a grocery store was opposite the office. Often I was the last one working, and when the grocery store closed at 8:00 pm it was my clue to go home.

One of those times I was so tired, I did not know what to do. My purse was empty, the car was close to empty and needed gas and there was no meal prepared for my children. At 8:00 pm the store opposite our office closed. I knew all the shops were then also closed. I could not stay there any longer for my own safety.

When I got home, Marguerite had received some money that day and she was preparing a meal for us. It was such a great relief. The Lord had taken care of us again. He is so faithful! I want to honor my family for always being there for us.

Without their support things would have been much more difficult. In many times of need, they stepped in and we survived the crisis. In my heart I believe that they will reap the harvest on the seeds that they have sown in our lives. But there were also many more times that I did not tell them about our needs. I felt so unworthy and would rather keep quiet than feeling like a burden for everybody. But in the midst of all of this, like the Israelite's clothes did not wear out in the desert, toiletries like deodorant, hairspray and even a luxury like perfume, miraculously kept on lasting.

I realize now that my children and I lived under a "poverty mentality". As we opened our hearts to the Lord, He revealed where all of this started for us, and over the years we were able to walk into freedom, step by step. John 10:10 is clear that the thief came to kill, steal and destroy, but Jesus came that we can have life and life in abundance. The enemy can only affect our lives where he has authority to do so, where there are "open doors" in our lives from generational sin or our own sin—or things that happened to us where we started to believe lies and live our lies as if those are truth. Jesus said that we'll know the Truth and the Truth will set us free. If I were giving advice about living the lies it would be this: Open your heart and ask Him for guidance. You don't need to focus on issues, focus on Him. He will show you. A man in our church once said to me - I've never seen a person with so much pain in her eyes. The most common comment I heard was: "Why are you so stressed, let me pray for you."

It happened a few times that I was invited to an event where the speaker was known as somebody who could prophecy. I wanted to get out of my financial situation and was hoping that he could show me the way to go. I was looking for solutions. A word of hope that things are going to change.

I was never disappointed with the outcome, though it sounded so unreachable. Back home I would write down what I heard, and for the next few days I read it over and over—also thanking the Lord for the plans He has for me.

This wonderful feeling only lasted for a week or two. When my situation did not change I was so confused. Gradually my mind would go another route. "You are just an ordinary person, a *nobody*. These promises are too big and amazing for you to receive. Rather, forget about it and focus on your job."

Scripture says: *"The worker deserves his wages"* 1 Tim. 5:18 (New International version). The scripture is truth, but it was not balanced with relationship with my Provider. I would work harder and harder while my stress was increasing, leaving me tired and burned out with no other goal in life but to survive. My trust was in my own works. My heart did not have revelation that God the Father is *my* Father. The issues of my heart consumed me. I didn't know that all I needed to do was to focus my eyes on the One who created everything, the One who knows the best way. I didn't know the value of living my life from my identity as Daughter. I was striving to have a place in life, not getting far.

# CHAPTER 16

## *Rest, Rest, Rest!*

There was a day in Marguerite's life, in 1997, a few years before she went to Toronto, Canada to attend the five-month School of Ministry, that she was crowned as Miss Universe South Africa first runner-up—It was a glamorous event. I remember sitting with tears in my eyes, deeply moved as I was watching my own daughter on stage—to see the confidence she had. But it was more than only confidence, it was His Presence that made the difference. She was so broken and to see what the Lord had already done in her heart at that point—it was a miracle.

I remember years ago when she was three years old, I would stop in front of the little shop in our small town. Instead of the two of us going in and buy bread, I would stay in the car and let her do it. In my mind there was a fear that if something happened to me, that she would not be able to help herself. It was important for me to let her be able to do things that I had not been able to do myself. She now is a compassionate mother for her and her husband's son, making sure not only his physical, but also his emotional and spiritual needs are met.

This is not where it ended. A few years later Lisl also did the School of Ministry. I could see how she was healed from many hurts and pains of the past. I once had a vision of Lisl praising and worshipping the Lord with hands in the air. That all came true. The change in her was incredible, and she is a wonderful mother to her children. I'm so proud of her!

Landi, my youngest, was also broken, insecure and very quiet because of all she went through as a child. She is tender hearted and cares about people, but she too could not stand up for herself. In her journey of receiving Revelation of the Father's Love and emotional healing, she also blossomed and has excelled as a mother and in her job. She's received several promotions in the corporate world. She is so precious to me!

Each of my three daughters has her unique journey with the Lord. Their relationship with the Lord today brings much joy to my heart. Because the four of us were each struggling with our own issues, we didn't really have deep relationships with one another, even though I deeply loved them. We still have a letter where Landi tried to bring us all together to talk and do fun things together. How we all wish we took her more seriously at the time.

But now all that has changed. Issues of the heart consumed us and took us away from focusing on what was really important. I'm so grateful for the restoration the Lord has brought to us as the journey continues—It's so true: As hearts heal relationships deepen.
Coming from the depths of extreme shyness, I think the change in myself was the most drastic. Never, ever would I (or my family!) think that I would be able to stand up before people and teach, not only in Afrikaans but also in English! Only the Holy Spirit could have done that!

Today this Revival is still impacting the world, and I believe it will never end, as people learn to pursue Him and value His Presence.

This is not only for preachers and leaders. It is for everyone, for you and me. My heart will forever be grateful for what the Lord has done!

Marguerite's life changed drastically, and one day she asked me to go with her to our church to attend a meeting about resting in the Lord's Presence. I did not know what it was about, and my first reaction was an emphatic "No!" I thought that was the end of it, but Marguerite had something else in mind. She kept on nagging 'til the point I agreed to go. (Thank you, Marguerite!) There was, however, one condition which I was very serious about. When we get there, just leave me alone, because you never know with Marguerite what she has in mind, especially when she thinks something is good for her mom! Coming from a traditional church, at that point the lifting of hands was still hard for me.

Marguerite is an amazing daughter and she did exactly what she promised. She left me all by myself in this 7000+ seat church while she went to worship at the front. I felt very uncomfortable, and if someone would even move into my direction, I would quickly move to the other side of the church. At last, after what felt like many hours, it was time to go home. I thought that was the end of it, but next time Marguerite asked again with "Mama, you know you need to go" and so I went again.

After a few times I very self-consciously went to the front, standing there, not even able to lift my hands, trying to sing. I say "sing" because it could not count for worship.

They placed high value on "resting" in His Presence, just being with the Lord, laying down your own agency and receiving from the Lord...positioning your heart to receive. That was what that specific meeting was for. Some people were sitting on their chairs. Others were even lying on the floor while worship music was playing; a time just to receive from the Lord.

So many incredible testimonies came from those times as the Lord spoke to people, showed them things; others received healing as the Lord brought truth to their hearts. Still others felt peace like they'd never felt before and there were also t estimonies where the Lord showed people what plans He had for them. It helped them to think bigger and dream bigger dreams. It was a very fruitful time.

The Holy Spirit is so faithful; I started to relax and eventually I also was lying on the floor where He could start working in my heart. Once I started relaxing in His Presence, I experienced Him in a different way, I became more aware that He was with me. *He is the God who is near* became revelation to me.

Everything started to change, and the need for Him became the focus of my life. They say you become like who you behold. The more you spend quality time with someone, the more you become like that person.

Taking time to be with Him completely transformed my life. It rescued me! During these times, He removed stress and revealed to me how He sees my situation. Truth I had in my head became heart revelation. I received healing and revelation. Above all, I received the unconditional love I so desperately needed. Revelation of His Love changes everything!

I was acting differently in certain situations than I had before. I started to go home on my lunch breaks only to rest in His Presence for a while. Doing this was so simple and yet I'd never heard about it before. I was used to praying in a one-way communication with the Lord, which is religion, not relationship. But in these moments of resting was the "other" side of the conversation. He was ministering to my heart, and it changed me forever. I knew there were scriptures about rest, but I was always so busy working only to survive, I did not understand them.
I was very good at the asking part, always a one-way conversation with the Lord. But now I was also resting in His Presence, listening to Him, receiving His Love.

This was a total shift in our relationship and there were even more benefits - my body also got the rest it so desperately needed. I had always been trying so hard to please God while He wanted me just to relax and trust Him. Ps. 46:10 describes it so beautifully – *"Be still and know that I am God."*

Sometimes I would sit on a chair if I didn't have much time, but most of the time I preferred a relaxed position on my bed. This is what Psalm 4:4 is talking about *"Meditate in your heart upon your bed and be still"*. (NASB). However, I must say there is something very special about lying on the floor in total surrender. During these times as I lay down my own agenda, I surrendered myself to the Holy Spirit, playing quiet worship music. Sometimes I preferred no music, only wanting to be in His Presence, focusing on His Love that He is so willing to pour into us. It took some time to quiet my thoughts down (it helps writing them down) and start focusing on Jesus, but the Holy Spirit is so faithful. He brings me so much peace and I know He is working in my heart, although many times I do not feel anything. Thankfully, it is not always about feeling but about a heart knowing that He is there. Psalm 23:2 *"He makes me lie down in green pastures; He leads me by still waters."* (NASB) In the beginning I was like Martha—always busy, busy, busy.

Surely it was the enemy trying to remind me of all the things I still had to do. (good to have a pen and paper ready to write these things down, so you know you won't forget and can focus on Him). I now realized that by giving Him that extra hour of my day, I could accomplish much more. Intimacy leads to fruitfulness. I also learned that the busier I was, the more I needed even just five minutes apart with Him during the day. The results of being in His Presence are so amazing!

At first I was like a dry sponge. If water is poured on it, there may be a little soft spot, but most of the water will roll off. If the sponge is soaked in water, it will become soft all over and eventually start dripping water. This is what happened to me. The more I spent time in His Presence, the softer my heart became. I was not the same person anymore. To spend time in His Presence became the most important part of my day. I also learned that if I want to keep something, I need to give it away. If I want to keep His love, I had to give it away—just asking Him to let His Love flow through me to people around me.

There was once a lady who was a very loud kind of person. I don't think she meant to be like that, but every time she spoke to me her voice was very harsh. Besides that, she was not sensitive in what she was saying to people. She was a Christian. It really upset me and I prayed about it. The Lord spoke very clearly to me: "Just allow My Love to flow through you to her." The next time I saw her, and every time after that, I quietly asked the Lord to let His Love flow through me to her. The results were amazing! She changed toward me, and since then we have become friends.

I was always frustrated when going to the bank or post office. There was, most of the time, a long line, and I had to wait while the tellers took their time. One day while standing there, the Holy Spirit quietly spoke to me—"Why don't you give My love away instead of complaining and wasting your time?" Wow! That was unexpected. But I chose to be obedient.

I asked the Lord to let His Love flow through me to every person in the room. At that moment I felt a change in the atmosphere and a big change in me also! We are carriers of His Presence.

From that day on, I decided to bless people, rather than curse them with negative thoughts. It is so weird, but now, most of the time, there will maybe be only one or two people in the line, but the moment I'm there, it seems they all start coming.

I sometimes went to pray for people in the hospital. Once there was a man by the name of Gerrie, who lost both of his legs in an accident. His wife then rejected him and kept their little girl away from him. When I met him the first time, he was very arrogant, telling me that he does not trust Christians and he did not want to talk to me. My heart was so full of compassion for him that I kept on going, deciding not to talk about Jesus 'til the time was right. I just loved him. Then one day out of the blue he looked at me saying, "I want what you have" and then I was able to lead him to the Lord. Not long after this, the matron of the hospital called me early one morning. She asked me to come and see Gerrie because there was a sudden a change in his condition, and he was about to die. When I got to the hospital, his family, including his wife and little girl, were there. But they all left the room when I came in. What a privilege it was to be with him, knowing he was on his way to his Heavenly home!

It is hard for our earthly minds to grasp the reality that the unseen world is more real than the seen world, but when we die, we step from one life into another—heaven or hell. It is the most important decision we'll ever make in our lives. It is not about whether you've had a good life or not. It is natural that you may not feel you need a Savior, but I urge you, reader, to ask Jesus to reveal Himself to you. First of all, God is love. Getting to know Him, you'll experience love you cannot even explain. There is a love need in our hearts that only God can fill, no human can. We are spiritual beings and our hearts are longing to connect with Him. There is a deep desire in there to receive love from the One who created us.

Ask Him now: "Jesus I want to know You. Thank you for paying the ultimate price for my sin on the Cross. I repent and ask Your forgiveness for all the things I've done wrong and the lies I believed about You. I receive Your forgiveness. I give my life to You. Holy Spirit, fill me in Jesus Name. Like Sarah, I want to know You."

# CHAPTER 17

## *Toronto!*

A few years went by, and all of a sudden Marguerite knew that the Lord wanted her to go to Toronto to do the five-month-long School of Ministry. It came as a huge shock to me, something I would never expect to happen. But I knew that if this was from the Lord nothing will stop it. In the natural it was completely impossible, but everything miraculously fell in place and before we knew it, it was time to go to the airport.
Lisl, Landi, my mother, sisters, myself and a lot of friends were there to say goodbye. Marguerite had many friends who really loved her. She waited 'til the announcement for boarding came and then started greeting everybody. Good thing at that point we still had a small airport. Doing it today may cause some problems!

Coming back home that evening there was a letter on my bed from her. She also left a little note for me. I've read it so many times during these years. At this point in time I feel that it is a word coming from the Father's heart to assure me these years later that He will be with her wherever she travels. 1 Chronicles 16:20–22: *"When they went from one nation to another and from one kingdom to another people, He permitted no man to do them wrong. Yes, He rebuked kings for their sakes saying, do not touch my anointed ones. And do my prophets no harm"(NKJV)*

I cried so much! Financially I felt like giving up. Marguerite as the eldest was my emotional support and now she was not there anymore. We all lived in one house and now her financial contribution was not there either. It was a price to pay for us all, but years later we all gained from her obedience.

I was too stressed to even focus on the Lord; old habits of

stress were knocking at my door. I can't imagine what I would have done if Lisl and Landi were not there for me. Jesus promised He will never leave us nor forsake us, and in His grace He showed me the way back to spend time in His Presence. That made all the difference.

God's plan for Marguerite to go to Toronto was very hard for us, but it would affected all of our lives in the years to come. New freedom has come to all of us. He knew what was best for us, though we couldn't it see at the time.

When Marguerite was in Toronto, we did not have skype and our only communication was when she called me, and that was always around midnight South African time. Fridays were our fax days when I would fax her a weekly letter.

One night she called me, and it was 1:00am when we finished the call. When I went back to my room, which I shared with Landi, I at first did not realize what was going on. I thought I was going to die! The whole room was covered in a thick mist with light beams in the one corner of the room. Everything was so peaceful. I could not understand what was going on. I've heard before when the Lord's Presence was so intense that a room was covered with mist. At that moment I was filled with an amazing peace. I immediately fell asleep. I realized that He filled our room with His wonderful manifest Presence. Today, I can see that picture in my mind so clearly.

We lived in a beautiful area, but it was also an area known for crime. One night I woke up and a soldier with full armor, like in the times of the Bible, was standing next to my bed. I had no fear. I knew the Lord sent His angel to assure us of His protection.

Another time I was in a different town at a function. It was a big venue. At one point, looking at the opposite wall, instead of a large wooden panel, I saw (with my eyes open) a beautiful river, surrounded with trees, grass and plants. A beautiful, peaceful scene. Nobody else could see it, but for the whole evening it was there for me. I asked the lady who sat next to me what she saw and she just saw the wall. It was so clear, as if I was physically there. I asked the Lord about it and what came to my mind was that this is what He has planned for me—His Peace and His rest and also His provision, always!

Sometimes the property business goes quiet. There can be various reasons for it, like banks becoming stricter in giving home loans, or seasonal, like during wintertime when people don't always want to go out. It was during such a season that I decided to try something else that would perhaps give me a better income. Instead of selling houses, I would now sell upmarket ovens. After meeting with the owner of the company, it all sounded good, and I decided to join them.

I did not really wait on the Lord, to hear what He would say about it. I was just so desperate for financial breakthrough. You would think, by now, I would have learned my lesson. Looking back I realize I was like the disciples who saw Jesus multiply the loaves and fish, and then the next time they needed to feed the people they did not know what to do. Scripture says Jesus said their hearts were still hardened. There was a part of my heart that some truth had not become revelation yet. Again, it's so important to have people speak into your life, asking the Lord what is best for your life. There is safety and wisdom in confirmation. It was a new challenge and I wanted to make it work. My sales were good, but very soon I realized that they expected me to do things that I was not comfortable with.

In the early morning, while people were getting ready for work, we were dropped off in a neighborhood, going from door to door trying to get appointments to demonstrate the ovens. I absolute hated doing that.

I had such an intense feeling of hopelessness, because I

desperately needed the money. But I've never done this before. I wouldn't be happy if somebody would come to my house early in the morning at such a busy hour of the day! I was so embarrassed, and deep within I could feel anger rising up. "Why must I do this? There must be a better way to earn money." What made it even worse was that the rest of the team was much younger than me.

A few days later I had sold three ovens to one client. But because it was not three different sales, my boss did not want to pay me the full commission. My trust in him was broken.

This owner of the company was, on one hand, very harsh with his team and even his wife, who did the administration for the company. On the other hand, he was declaring what a wonderful Christian he was. While in a meeting he set up for my friend and me, he told us that if he could have more people in his team like the two of us, he would be able to earn enough money so that he could stop working himself.

Somebody at church told him that he needed to be in ministry. I had no peace about it, something just did not feel right to me. I felt that enough was enough. I decided to go back to my friends at the Real Estate Agency who kept on asking me to join them again. This was a breakthrough moment for me—that I actually could say enough was enough.

# CHAPTER 18

## *My first son!*

When my children were happy, I was the first to know but when they had problems, I was also the first one they told, which I appreciated. To be mom and to be dad as well was not always easy. Additionally, the stress of nearly always being financially strapped put a huge burden upon me. Many times I felt like giving up.

So many times I went to work early and came back late. I would walk the last mile with a client helping them find their dream house. It happened that other agents would give up on a client, but I would keep on until, in the end, I had a signed contract. That always was such a good feeling!

After five months, Marguerite came back from Toronto. I was so excited, waiting at the airport hours too early. But my joy was not to last. An hour or two after her arrival, she told me that she was leaving again soon, as they had asked her a few days earlier to be a leader at the school in Toronto for two more five month sessions. In that moment, I knew my daughter's future would be in another country.

That afternoon while preparing dinner, with tears and these thoughts going through my mind, the Lord spoke very clearly to me. "Release your daughter. I will take care of you". At that moment, I knew I had to release her. I had peace about it, although it was still not easy to take her to the airport after just two weeks—again.

I've found that if I trust Him, the Lord will never let me down. In between the school sessions Marguerite was always able to come home. He provided money for her plane ticket, which was a huge miracle every time. Her whole journey—going to Toronto and the money for tickets—was possible because, in her own walk, she started to receive revelation of His Kingdom finance.

During this time, Marguerite felt that the Lord said that it was time for me to quit being a real estate agent. But I was too afraid of taking such a big step. How would we survive? One day I decided to see the pastor who was in charge of the Prophetic team at our church. To my surprise he said the same thing to me. The Lord also showed him a beehive with one bee standing against the wall. With the crossing of his arms, he was saying enough is enough! But still, I did not have the courage and faith to give it up. Shortly after that I signed six contracts for the month, but four of them, in a very strange way, did not go through. Then I knew that the time had come to make a change.

A very well-known guitarist in South Africa asked me if I could manage his bookings. This included travelling all over the country. Again it was something new to me, but because it included some travel, I decided to go for it.

During Marguerite's time in Toronto as leader, she met the man who would be her husband, Andy. He is from the UK and was doing the same five month school she had been doing previously.

After she completed her time as a leader and Andy finished his school, they both stayed on at the church. Marguerite was offered a job at the church and miraculously got a work permit! The lady who worked with the new staff encouraged her to apply for a volunteer kind of visa since she was from Africa. It was hard for people from Africa to get work visas in Canada. Marguerite felt the Lord encouraged her to apply for hard-to-get work permit since she'd been offered a full time job, and she got it. Andy was asked to be a pastoral intern and helped coordinate conferences for the church. They started dating.

There was one special call. One morning, at 5:00 am my cellphone rang. I was very tired and I switched it off. It rang again and I did the same thing, too tired to give attention to the "unknown" on the screen.

At 9:00 am while in a business meeting, it rang again, but this time I just knew this was not an everyday call. I quickly went outside to take the call. I was so surprised to hear Andy's voice, and at the same time I
was very nervous knowing that I had to talk to him in English. I wonder which one of us was the most nervous! So there, while sitting on the green grass underneath a huge shadow tree, he asked the "big question" and I knew it was right. I had so much peace about it, just knowing that he would be a son to me.

They came back to South Africa to get married, and I met my new son-in-law face-to-face, just a week before the wedding. Andy was not a total stranger to me though, since we had a number of conversations on the phone during the engagement. They got married in a beautiful venue called The Farm Inn, a wildlife sanctuary in Pretoria, South Africa. The thatch roofs of this venue, together with wild animals like lions, cheetahs, giraffes and several more, made it a real African experience for those coming from abroad. What made it more special was that the accommodation, as well as the chapel, was part of the venue.

On that very day, I got a phone call in the morning saying that a big property deal on which I was working did not go through. It was a huge disappointment on such a beautiful day. I don't know how I would have been able to process all of this if I hadn't known the Lord. I was able to release it to Him and was able to fully embrace the beauty of the day.

Marguerite, together with bridesmaids Lisl and Landi and myself, was getting ready in one of the chalets.
The hairdresser was not in a hurry and took his time. We all got a reality check when the wedding planner came running in saying we are now beyond fashionably late! Yes, Marguerite was 40 minutes late for her wedding.

We all started running. Lisl and Landi were leading, followed by the bride holding up her beautiful dress. Next in the line, I was followed by the clothing designer and his assistant. Marguerite had been in the fashion industry before she went to Toronto and had modeled, many times, his clothing. Marguerite's flower girls were from different ethnic backgrounds portraying her heart for the nations. These men, making jokes while we were running, were the reason for all of us laughing as we reached the chapel—only to be stopped by the photographer waiting for us!

This was a good thing, giving us time to collect ourselves. I was so nervous in giving my daughter away. At that moment all the tension was gone. I was able to smile while walking with her down the aisle, giving her away to a smiling bridegroom waiting on her!

The ceremony started with worship, which was a new experience for most of the guests in the wedding ceremony. This caused a totally different atmosphere—entering into His presence. After that, a pastor and his wife from America spoke, while the ceremony was officiated by a pastor from South Africa.

Then it was time for taking photos. What made everything more special were the lion cubs that Andy and Marguerite were able to hold in their arms. It all took place in a beautiful garden. A bright sunny day in spring. Everything was just perfect!

By this time everyone was hungry, and we could enjoy a

wonderful evening with music and good food, lots of laughter and lots of fun!

After they flew home again, Andy, as a caring son-in-law would do, sometimes emailed me. I so appreciated it, but there was only one problem. He could not speak Afrikaans, so he did it in English, which meant that I had to reply in English! I think it was the Holy Spirit who gave me this idea: I would write him a letter in Afrikaans then asked Lisl or Landi to do the translation. That worked out perfectly!

Shortly after this, Marguerite mentioned to John and Carol Arnott from Catch the Fire Ministries that I was serious about taking time resting in the Lord's presence and told them of all the Lord had done in my heart. They then decided to ask me to be their National Coordinator for South Africa. This was an amazing opportunity for me. I would still organize events for the musician I worked for but would also have time to speak to people about our ministry events. First though, I had to do the one-month International School of Leaders in Toronto. I was so excited! I longed for the ministry that I was going to receive, and it would also be my first experience abroad. For Marguerite, having her mother coming there was like a dream come true.

After John and Carol asked me to be their coordinator, they visited South Africa. They brought me a "Soaking Kit" as a gift. For me it was one of the most precious gifts I had ever received. It was not only a gift; the message it contained would have eternal value.

Inside the kit were CD's, DVD's and other material explaining the importance of being in His presence. It explained how to come into His presence and gave the scriptural foundations behind each teaching. It was not about "jump up and go" but rather taking time to receive more. It was about spending time and "being with Him" rather than "doing" something. He sets the agenda. It was about a time when we receive from Him.

Before I could do the school, Andy and Marguerite decided to go for an opportunity at Shiloh Place in the USA. For Marguerite that was no problem at all; I could visit them after I was through with school. Before I left for Canada, Lisl organized a farewell dinner at a restaurant. It was an amazing evening with family and friends. It now became reality that I was going abroad; it was not only a dream anymore. My emotional state was one of mixed feelings. On the one hand I was so excited to go, and on the other hand I was torn, thinking about saying goodbye to nearly everything and everyone I had known. Especially, leaving my mother as well as Lisl and Landi was a big deal for me. But the Lord had provided for everything. This was to be an incredible moment in my life.

I'd never been overseas before, and I was so nervous. What made it worse was that I had to go via busy Heathrow Airport in London, which was scary to me. But, even in things like getting a seat on the plane, the Lord was so faithful.

# CHAPTER 19

## *Opportunity of a lifetime*

Seated next to me on the flight leaving South Africa was a young man who spoke Afrikaans, like me, and he was so helpful. At Heathrow, he went with me as far as he could and then showed me the way to my gate, where I met with another South African couple who were also on their way to Toronto. Everything went smoothly, no problems at all!

I was very nervous while going through customs. I'd never done it before, and I did not know what to expect. People back home were praying for me and I credit that with everything going fine; the customs agents were very kind to me. I was so relieved when I got my suitcases without waiting very long. Going through the doors, I immediately saw Madeleine, the pastor's wife and her daughter waiting for me. I could finally relax for the first time, knowing I was in Toronto at last and I'd made it!

The first weekend, I stayed with the pastor's family, whom I had met before when they were on a visit to South Africa. When I opened my suitcase, tears filled my eyes when I spotted two envelopes tucked in between my clothes. This was a special way of Lisl and Landi saying goodbye to me and assuring me of their love and prayers. I still treasure those letters!

In the meantime Marguerite started calling from the USA. She wanted to make sure everything was fine. She knew that this was a first experience for me in a totally different situation.

The school started on Monday morning. The students were from countries all over the world and most of them were pastors and leaders of their churches. I realized, "I am none of that!", but the thought was not to consume me. I had not much time to dwell on it because everybody on staff was so kind and wanted to chat since they all knew Marguerite. And they all loved her. My daughter had left grace in her wake! She even asked a young man on staff to give me a hug every time he saw me, which he faithfully did!

During the first week of the school, Marguerite surprised me with a huge parcel in the mail. Her gift to me was nice clothes and other goodies she knew I would need. I cried again; my children are so special to me!

At the time, the school, as well as the accommodation, was in a "renovated" warehouse located close to the church.

At the end of the first week, a man from South Africa, whom I'd met before, also joined us. While she was still in South Africa, Marguerite had been part of his prophetic group. A sudden feeling of unworthiness came over me. This school is for pastors and leaders. I have no right to be here! What will he think of me? The moment I saw him I started explaining that I was invited to do school.

He, a wonderful man of God, just looked at me. At that moment I could feel that it was okay that I was there. The Lord had given me this opportunity, and I wanted all that He had for me.

Marguerite likes surprises, and she's an expert at making them happen! Everybody except me knew she was coming to visit me the second weekend I was there. I couldn't believe my eyes when I saw her. I could only stare at her, as if she was someone from another world! I thought I would only see her and Andy after the school in the USA—and here she was, right in front of me!

While in Toronto I received a lot of prayer ministry and many emotional hurts of the past were healed. I processed a lot of pain and received Truth from the Lord. It was a time of healing, a time of renewing my mind and understanding more of who I am as a daughter of the Father and a recipient of what Jesus had done on the Cross for me. As I was filled afresh with the Holy Spirit, my hunger for His presence increased the more.

It was such an amazing time, making new friends in a totally new environment. Because the church and our living quarters were so close to the airport, I enjoyed sitting outside during breaks watching all the planes, wondering about their destinations. Everything was so new and exciting to me.

The school started with sessions about "Hearing God's Voice". I knew He speaks to us through His Word and also through spontaneous thoughts coming to our minds, but for the first time I learned that there are three voices speaking to us all the time; God, the enemy and our own thoughts.

So often in the past a negative thought would come to my mind. It was disturbing because I couldn't understand why I was thinking that way.

I would judge myself, asking the Lord for forgiveness. I then realized it came from the enemy. I needed to "switch channels" in my mind...choose to think about something different. But it was also important to learn that as soon as I start meditating on those thoughts it becomes a sin. I learned to evaluate my thoughts, saying to myself: "Would Satan say kind and encouraging things to me? Surely not!" If it was beyond my ability to be thinking that way, then who else could it be but God? The opposite is also true—would God speak such negative thoughts to me? Surely not! It took some time for me to realize that my focus is not to be on what comes to my mind but more what I am doing with those thoughts.

The enemy will always accuse and condemn, while the Holy Spirit convicts and comforts. When ungodly thoughts keep on bombarding your mind, then there may be a deep place that needs healing.

I also learned how to deal with the hurts and pain from the past. So many people go through life, not understanding why they feel a certain way or act in a certain way. So often the roots of those negative things can be found in their past, before they reached the age of five, or even as far back as before birth, while they were in their mother's womb. It has been scientifically proven that babies in the womb know how their parents feel about them. Where there is a fruit, there will always be a root. We don't need to dig for stuff, just ask the Holy Spirit and He will show you, when the time is right. His timing is best. We just need to have open hearts.

There were many things that happened in my life that caused me much pain. During ministry, the Holy Spirit took me back to many of those situations, to the point where I could feel the pain again. If the pain is still there, then a hurt is still affecting your life, and there is usually a lie underneath, supporting it and keeping the pain alive. As soon as I asked Jesus to effect a situation with His healing Love, I was able to release the pain to Him. During these healing times my mind was being renewed with His truth. There was a grace after each session for healing in the area the speaker had been speaking of. Much prayer had gone into this school long before we even arrived. Our hearts were ready. I was desperate for breakthrough.

After these healing moments, I was still able to remember may past and the things that had happened, but the pain was gone. The Holy Spirit showed me many things that I did not even remember anymore, but that were affecting my life. These moments were very deep and so painful, but the relief and peace I felt afterwards was worth it all. I felt like a new person!

Pain and love cannot be in the same place in our hearts. As the pain was released, His love filled those places. I felt so much lighter!

The Lord dealt with us in different ways. Some of the students couldn't stop crying during these sessions. There was so much hurt and pain to be dealt with. Many times the Holy Spirit does great healing on the inside without any manifestation on the outside. It is about the heart.

This kind of ministry was not new to me. A few months before the school, while visiting, Marguerite ministered to me. There was one specific area where I really felt that I needed breakthrough. I had the mindset that I was not good enough, and that was why men often did not treat me well. Because I could not stand up for myself and I didn't know my worth or value, they would walk all over me, hurting me with harsh words. I had enough, I wanted, I needed, to be free from this.

At that point in time there was a man whose event bookings I did. It was very easy for him to be rude to me, and he took pleasure in doing so.

Marguerite ministered to me and the Holy Spirit took me back to a situation long ago that was the root of all of this. I shared with the Lord all I felt in that memory and was able to get in touch with the pain, and as I was giving it all to Jesus, the pain lifted. We asked Jesus what lies I believed about myself in that situation. He revealed the lies and I was able to forgive each man who treated me badly, and I repented for judging them. I broke my agreement with those lies and also repented for even receiving them. I didn't know I was believing those lies until the Lord revealed them to me. I was amazed at how they affected my life. I then asked Jesus what He thought about me, especially in those situations. His truth replaced the lies I believed.

The change was instant! I was no longer insecure in that area, and I knew that I was worthy to be treated well by everybody. The change in the rude man toward me was incredible—no more was the enemy able to steal from me. His legal rights in that situation were taken away from him that day.

But, I still had another situation to deal with. Financially, life was not easy. A certain man's heart was to help me, but at the same time he would say things like: "You know you do not have money, you are poor. How are you going to survive?" He didn't care if he was saying it in front of other people! He wanted to be seen as the good man caring about this poor woman. This was familiar to me. My first husband would do the same, saying negative things about me to my parents so that he would sound like the good man.

I worked for the money he paid me. Therefore, he felt he could just slime me and crush me with his words and not even think twice about it.

Before Marguerite ministered to me, I always kept quiet instead of asking what the Word of God says about our needs—that all my needs are met. It was as if I was in agreement with this man and with the identity of poverty and couldn't stand up for myself. After ministry, something rose up in me. "I'm not going to be embarrassed anymore." It took a long time for him to stop doing it, because it already was a habit. Every time he would do it, I cancelled his words in Jesus name, and I told him that what he was doing was cursing me. His words were words of death and not life. As Proverbs 18:21 says, *"Life and death is in the power of the tongue"*. Our words are powerful.

The last week of the school was about the prophetic. I did not know what to expect. I was nervous but also excited. I wanted to know more about it. Ivan and Isabel Allum did the prophetic teachings. They were amazing! I could not stop listening; hunger for more of Him was stirring in my heart. They carried the love of the Father in a tangible way. The way they talked about the Lord, their relationship with Him so touched my heart. I wanted to know more; I wanted to know Him more! At the end, the students had to prophecy over each other, and the Lord really came through for me. At first I was very nervous but the Holy Spirit is so faithful, He will never let you down if you trust in Him. One of the most important things I realized was that prophecies were for things to happen in future. It was God's promises for His children. I started believing that He has a plan and a future for me. I was so excited about these Promises of the Lord that I decided to believe them and make them my own. Back home I would read them over and over, meditate on them and challenge circumstances with them. Some of them have already come to pass while for me, the most important ones are happening now, 11 years after I received them.

For years I felt different, I did not always like the things my sisters liked (like dancing!). Surely there had to be something wrong with me. This is what Isabel said to me: "This is what the Lord says: There has been times in your life that the enemy tried to make you believe there is something wrong with you. You are a wonderful woman and a very strong woman. There is a strength in you that can do anything. You have the strength of a bear and the strength of a lion always in you". Those words were words of life to me, and that's the beauty and power of the prophetic gift. I never saw myself like that. Those words awakened what God has put inside of me.

They also said that the Lord will open doors to do things that I never did before. It all started in the few years that I was Coordinator for Catch the Fire Ministries. I received training and as the Coordinator was leading my National Team, and I did teachings in English. I'll never forget Lisl's face; she was there when I did the first teaching about "Soaking in His Presence" in English during an event in Cape Town. She immediately called Marguerite in the USA to tell her about it!

She said she couldn't believe it. I remember first of all saying to the audience, "I cannot speak English but the Holy Spirit can!"

At the end of the school, another surprise was waiting on me. Marguerite unexpectedly arrived for my graduation. I so appreciated her for doing that! To share this event with my daughter meant so much to me and there was also another benefit—we could fly together to the USA, which meant no stress for me!

Coming to their home, Andy was on top of the shed fixing the roof, and, outside on the fence, a huge banner with "Welcome to America Mamma". Inside the house, in my room, were flowers and balloons with yellow roses. Both of us were so surprised. I can't relate what that meant to me. It was so special! Thank you, Andy!!

There was another surprise waiting for me - I thought I had enough prayer ministry for one season, but Marguerite had more in mind. At first I did not want to go, but I realized it would be for my own benefit. I had ministry for another day at Shiloh Place, and I still remember Marguerite's face when she came to pick me up that afternoon—"Mamma, it's gone!" She then explained that there was still something, she could still see some pain in my eyes. But that day that "something" was healed. The hurt and pain was reflecting no more. I received deeper revelations of my Heavenly Father's love for me. The issues of the heart are like an onion. We deal with it layer after layer. The Lord knows when we are ready for the next layer. We don't have to dig for it, we just need to have an open heart for Him. Healing to our hearts can come in many different ways. I have received much healing and revelation sovereignly from the Lord while spending quality time with Him...at other times during personal prayer ministry, or people praying for me, or sometimes while reading my Bible or listening to a sermon.

For many years now I've had a friend, Alida. She's a woman of faith, with many years in ministry experience. During difficult times she and her husband Johan have always been there for me. During those difficult years she so many times prayed for me and supported me. I could not have walked my way through this life entirely on my own; no one can, and, thanks to Jesus, none of us need walk alone.

During my visit Marguerite and I went on a three day cruise to the Bahamas. She saved her last Canadian tax return for our trip, which put a smile on her face, as we both received so much healing in Toronto, and now her Canadian tax return is paying for our trip together! This was a first experience for both of us.

Marguerite, in her excitement, had already started taking pictures with our suitcases still at the front door! While on our way, it was fascinating for me, coming from South Africa, to pass the "Miami" sign. We drove many hours to the port. Wow! It felt so unreal! Because our cruise ship would leave the following morning, we spent the night in a hotel. It was the most fascinating feeling, leaving the harbor that day. We were standing outside on the deck, amazed by all the Lord has done. Just a few years ago this moment was absolutely impossible in our little worlds. Our worlds were so incredibly small, and here we were... The goodness of God is beyond description!!

I can still feel this big cruise ship ploughing through the water, and in the distance all one could see was the ocean.

Everything was new for us. We did not want to miss anything. We went to all the restaurants, we ate all the time and loved it—after all, it was all included! There is a story of a man who took his family by ship to another country and they took crackers and a small amount of non-perishable food for their journey. The last day, as the ship arrived at their destination, he asked how much it would have been for him and his family to eat the food on the ship. The reply was that all the food, every day, was included in his ticket, but he didn't know it. That is like our relationship with the Lord. We only enjoy the crumbs until we receive revelation of all that is available for us in Him, in His Kingdom, here, now.

We enjoyed visiting all the cute little shops and even went for a treat at the Beauty Spa! That night I was too excited to sleep, and, while looking through the porthole, saw another ship not far from us going in the opposite direction. Maybe I saw someone who, just like me, could not sleep, because I saw the flash of a camera toward our ship.

We spent one day at the Bahamas. The turquois color of the ocean, the white sand and lots of palm trees were so amazingly beautiful! We were in a totally different world, an exotic world. Someday I would love to do that again.

During my time in Toronto, and also with our visit to the Bahamas, the Lord showed His Love as a Father to His children in a very special way. He provided for the tickets and the cruise in amazing ways. I was His daughter, and He was proving to be a Father who gives His children good gifts.

# CHAPTER 20

## *Reality back home*

The time came for me to head back to South Africa. I was looking forward seeing everybody again after nine weeks. At the same time, I knew I was going to face some financial realities. Although I had no debt, I needed to pay rent for our apartment.

Soon after I got home, a book arrived in the mail from Marguerite. She felt that Bill Johnson's book "When Heaven Invades Earth" would be very helpful for me, and she was spot on.

When the end of the month came, I still had no money for rent. Not even part of it. For the first time in my life I could understand what "let Your Kingdom come" really means. It was now or never and I was seriously not to going let go of this new-found truth and all that the Lord had done in my heart during my time in North America. I said—"Let Your Kingdom come, Your will be done in my finances. There's no lack in heaven, there shouldn't be on earth, therefore I will have the rent for this month."

While my landlord was patient, I was holding unto God's promise, not giving up. Over and over I said to myself, Jesus is not a liar, He will do what He has promised. I visualized it, meditated on it. I believed it with my whole heart. It was not anymore words spoken into the air, hoping that God somewhere up there will listen to it. My mind was being renewed, as Romans 12:2 explains.

A few days before the end of the month, two ladies whom I met for the first time felt that the Lord told them to give me money, and my rent was paid. This was His supernatural provision. From that day on, if I needed something I would let His Kingdom come on the situation and sure enough, He always came through. He provided through the work I did and also through other ways. He is not limited. We need to do our part and apply what He teaches us about Kingdom finance and believe that He is who He says He is.

As Coordinator for Catch the Fire Ministries, it was time to start organizing events in South Africa, building a National Team to spread the message—for lives to be changed. It was my passion! I enjoyed every moment of it. When I travelled with the musician all over the country doing concerts in churches, I had many opportunities to speak to people about our events. Because it was my passion, it was not difficult for me to do. There were religious people who were not interested. But there were many who had a hunger for more of the Lord and wanted to know more. I felt that the events I booked for the musicians were a vehicle to share with people what the Lord has done in my life. These were some precious moments in my life.

More teams started to come from Toronto. Usually, when it was an International School of Leaders, Duncan and Kate Smith would come with their team. They called me their "South African Mama". When it was a "Soaking in His Presence" weekend, Jeremy and Connie Sinnott would be the leaders, also coming from Toronto. They gave training for my team and me. We instantly connected with each other. On these events I could spend more time with them, getting to know them better. We had a wonderful relationship and they supported me in everything. I had the privilege to do this for seven years. We had numerous events in different parts of the country.

As Coordinator I had to go to all the events that I organized. It was a huge responsibility, and a lot of work. During the day I would do events for my musicians, and many times 'til very late at night I worked on CTF's events. I had no problem doing that because it was my passion. Not only did I have to take care of all the details of an event, also included was doing the research and booking for accommodation, local flight tickets, meals, liaison with local churches and host churches, the team, etc. Lisl helped me with the local flights and relieved some pressure.

Once I had six pastors who came from Zimbabwe, Zambia, Kenya and Uganda. They arrived in Pretoria by bus without knowing where they were going to stay. It was a long trip and they had no money left for food and accommodation. But they had faith. They knew that the Lord will provide for them. There is nothing complicated in their faith, they simply believed the Word and acted on what the Lord said. I was able to rent a large apartment so that they all could be together and made sure that they had more than enough to eat. They were so full of joy, like one happy family together! For the time and even afterwards, they called me their "Mama". After the event I received a few invitations to visit their churches, but due to circumstances at the time, I was not able to go.

Being the Coordinator was far more than just organizing the events. I'd never been on a ministry team before, praying for people. I had no self-confidence to do that, but for me this felt like a safe environment to minister to people and to pray with them. Gradually my confidence increased in praying for people. I had compassion and empathy with those who carried pain. It was amazing to see people set free from difficulties of the past.

I so enjoyed connecting with the attendees as they arrived, encouraging them. Most of them did not really know what to expect; they came because they had a hunger for more of the Lord. Some were curious and many were broken, tired from coping and even burnt out. For many "Resting (soaking) in His Presence", was a first experience.

One time there was an elderly lady, a very sincere Christian from another town. With the first session of "Soaking in His Presence", she was upset because she was not familiar with that terminology and wanted to go home, on the spot. I spent time with her, encouraged her to stay and first experience it for herself. That woman totally changed! By the end she was so full of joy and just wanted to stay in His Presence!

There was also a pastor from a church a few hours away from Cape Town, where this particular event was held. He was very excited because a pastor friend of his from the same town had invited him to come. His first reaction was the same as the elderly lady's, except that he was even more upset and made it clear that he was going to leave. I had a conversation with him and, as with the lady, he promised to stay a little longer. He did not just stay "a little longer", he stayed four more days till the end of the event! He was so on fire after receiving much healing from pain of the past and experiencing the presence of the Lord in a deeper way. The first Sunday back in his own church, he shared what the Lord had done, and his whole church was set on fire for the Lord!

Being the Coordinator for CTF was a wonderful time in my life, a time that I will never forget. I will always be thankful for John and Carol giving me that opportunity. It was an incredible blessing in my life. Thank you John and Carol, I so appreciate you!

# CHAPTER 21

## *"Life and death is in the power of the tongue"*

As Lisl and Landi started working, each of the three of us were responsible for her own expenses. That worked out perfectly for us, as we shared everything. By that time each of them had her own car. When they went out with friends, they had to give me a missed call when they reached their destinations. When they were on their way back, they had to do it again.

It was not that I did not trust them. There were many robberies and hijackings on that notorious route. I could not sleep until they were home again. I always said that the most beautiful sound for me was when I heard the key in the front door. I then knew they were back. I know the right thing was to give it all to the Lord and to trust Him. He promised to send His angels to protect them. I prayed, but I still worried. One day it was like a revelation that I realized that I had to trust that He will do what He has promised in His Word. He also reminded me of His promise of protection that He gave me years ago in the little "rondavel" after my first divorce.

Finally, I knew that if I really trusted the Lord for keeping my children safe, I could ask Him for that and then go to sleep. Worry was not faith. Although I prayed and asked Him to send His angels, according to Psalm 91, to protect them, I was still speaking and acting in fear. In His love and grace He showed me to meditate on who He is and on His faithfulness. He reminded me of the many times in the past that He protected us, and finally I got it. It now shifted from knowing with my head to believing with my heart for this thing, too. I was able to fully trust Him in the area of protecting my precious daughters, too.

Now with my children so far away, it doesn't matter whether I'm in South Africa or the USA, at least one of them is thousands of miles away. Every time the enemy tries to put fear unto me, I start focusing on Jesus, resting in Him for a few minutes, breaking the agreement with fear, stepping into His Peace. It works every time!

I am also convinced that my situation could have been totally different if I'd, earlier in my life, received revelation, not only head knowledge, of the power of our words as it is said in Proverbs 18:21: "*Life and death are in the power of the tongue, and those who love it will eat it's fruit*". Out of a place of fear I said so many negative things about myself and my situation. Now I'm very mindful of my words. With who do I want to agree? The accuser—or the Holy Spirit.

It is so easy to speak negative words over yourself or allow others to speak them over you (or you over them!). In reality, these are curses flying all over, touching people's lives negatively. I can still remember negative things people spoke over me when I was in school. For many years I believed the lies and acted accordingly.

People also used to say how shy I was. Somehow I took the identity of shyness on me. In every situation I would stand back because "I'm too shy". My true personality could not hold me back. It was my beliefs and confessions made by me and others that held me back. That withheld me from doing sports and taking part in normal school activities. Today, after learning to spend time in His presence, I'm a totally different person. My family cannot believe I'm the same person as years ago!

Speaking positive words, especially when you speak the Word over people, has the opposite outcome, a positive outcome, because there is a promise—that the angels are sent to make it come through. I daily decree Scriptures over my children, my grandchildren and my family because I know their lives will be positively touched by that. But if I were to say negative things, surely the enemy and his demons would also see that those come to pass.

In the past I always felt so unworthy. If someone would give me a compliment, my response immediately would be negative. For example: "I like your dress", I would reply something like, "Oh, thank you, you know it is only homemade." I had to learn to accept compliments and thank people for their good intentions.

I really appreciate and respect elderly people. But for me, now getting older, I was looking at myself as unworthy in the eyes of the world, not to be respected by people anymore. One day the Holy Spirit showed me how the enemy wanted to rob me from my destiny. This was all in my mind, because in reality I receive so much love and kindness from people. I love to be with them. The Lord has promised me so much more and I don't want to miss out on anything! I'm worthy to be loved and to love others.

# CHAPTER 22

## *Wedding in the mountains!*

As little birds leave their nests, the time came for my Landi to get married. I will always remember one evening Laurence came to visit her. I was in my bedroom, and the next moment he was standing in my door, tears rolling down his face. I did not know what was going on. He asked me to forgive him for difficulties that they had in their relationship before. This meant so much to me, and I knew deep inside that this young man is someone very special, with a gentle heart. He excels in all he does; he is very gifted. I was not surprised when he called me one morning from work, asking the "big" question!

A few months later, they had a very intimate wedding of only close family, a few hours away, high up in the mountains. The venue was only reachable by 4x4's. Marguerite came all the way from the USA to do the ceremony. It was very special!

The evening before the wedding, we had a family barbecue. This gave us the opportunity to build relationship with our new family. After the barbecue we went to our beautiful cabin. It was so fun to sit back and watch my daughters playing card games with my mother and my sister. There was lots of laughter. Needless to say, we did not go to bed early!

Early the next morning Lisl and my mom went for a walk in the bush. They quickly returned when suddenly baboons were barking behind them. Instead of a nice and peaceful walk, it became a race back to the cabin, fast, leaving those baboons far behind!

It is a beautiful thing for me to see—all the Lord has done in Landi's life. We've been through so much together. I know my decisions in life affected my children in a negative way, but when we see the Lord's faithfulness, as we turn to Him, we find

Him already waiting for us. There is nothing like the Grace of Jesus Christ. In Him we are new creations. The old has gone and the new has come. He is with us every step of the journey. We just need to ask Him, to open our hearts and allow the Great Physician to work in our hearts.

What a moment it was, seeing Landi walking down the aisle at her open-air wedding. The views were breathtaking. My baby curly-haired girl had grown up into a beautiful woman. My miracle child, and at that moment in time, my joy.

Now it was Lisl, myself and my Siamese/Persian blue-eyed cat, who thinks he owns the property, living together...but not for very long.

I organized a Catch the Fire International School of Leaders in Pretoria where John and Carol Arnott met Lisl. She helped them and their team during their time in South Africa. They saw the potential in her, and after the School they invited Lisl to do the School of Ministry in Toronto. Then, in Cape Town I had again a prompting in my spirit to take Lisl along with me as I worked. After all, she was brilliant with the kinds of things I was doing, so we went together. It was there and then that plans fell in place for her. Catch the Fire Leaders, Duncan and Kate Smith, who lead the School, fell in love with Lisl and saw the incredible potential in her. They invited her too. Within months she was on her way to do the School of Ministry and, at the same time, be an Intern for Jeremy and Connie Sinnott at CTF in Toronto. They immediately saw who Lisl was, brilliant and gifted. Jeremy and Connie are so precious to me. They promised to take care of Lisl and that's exactly what they did. They treated her as a daughter, watching over her and making it easier for me to let go of my little girl.

I will always remember coming home from the airport that evening. It was one of the loneliest feelings of my life. Painfully lonely. Reality struck me for the first time in my life that I was alone. From now on, my children will only visit me. Mine will never be the home where they live again. I had to get used to my new situation. There was no need to get dinner ready for somebody coming home after work anymore. I can eat what I want, whenever I want...nobody to consider anymore. Suddenly everything was different.

It took some time, but after a while I got used to this "new freedom" and, knowing that my children were all happy, I started enjoying it. The only person I had to check on was myself. Landi and Laurence came to my home for lunch every Sunday. I prepared them a nice meal, and for the rest of the week I did not concern myself much with their lives. It was now a new season in my life, and I decided to spend more time with the Lord. I was still very busy organizing concerts for the musicians, travelling all over the country. I spent many hours in the car. I learned that although I was in the car with the radio on, I could easily "switch channels" in my mind and focus on the Lord, resting in His presence, having communion with Him.

I learned the value of, at any time, asking the Holy Spirit to release His peace and His presence in my heart and in that car, everywhere I went. It is amazing how different one acts in situations when aware of His presence. Jesus promised He will always be with us and always means *always*, whether we feel it or not!

I like reading Christian books that I feel the Lord lead me to read. I not only read them, I live them. I have received many revelations through these books. There is one specific book, "Hosting the Presence" by Bill Johnson. I take it with me wherever I go. That book has already made a few trips with me between the USA and South Africa! I meditate on the Truths. Sometimes the renewing of the mind takes time, grasping the truth to be able to live it, not just knowing about it. There is a big difference.

A few weeks after Lisl left, Laurence and Landi's little boy Elijah was born. My first grandchild! I remember clearly that evening in the hospital. I took our little baby in my arms, looked at him and blessed him. He was so beautiful! Afterwards, whenever he visited me I would play Arthur Burk's Baby Blessing CDs while he was sleeping, making sure our little baby gets as many blessings as possible. Also when we call him by his name, we declare over him the meaning of "Elijah". That is so amazing!

In the meantime Marguerite got her citizenship in the United States. We decided to apply for my green card. I was glad that it just happened that Marguerite was in South Africa when I had to go for all the medical tests. Having her with me made all the difference.

# CHAPTER 23

## *Wedding via skype!*

It took about two years, but Lisl, now also in America, met "Mr. Right", Daniel, and not long after that, they decided to get married. This time I didn't get a phone call. Daniel sent me a beautiful email, asking me if he could marry my daughter. (I still have that letter, it is very precious to me!) There was only one problem. Because of her visa, if they were to marry in South Africa, she had to stay there for several months. If they chose America, I couldn't be there because my green card application was still in process, which meant I could not travel there until the process was finalized.

It was a very strange feeling for me, as her mother, not to be, in any way, part of my daughter's beautiful day. I'm so glad Marguerite and Andy were able be there for her. One wonderful lady, Martha, offered to do a wedding shower for the wedding. I attended via Skype.

Marguerite tried her best to let me be part of it all. The day when Lisl bought her dress I watched it all on Skype and gave my input. It made not being there easier for me. In some way I felt part of it. Thank you Marguerite!
Seeing how Lisl has blossomed so moved my heart. It takes one person to see someone's potential and call it forth. My little quiet girl who once stood in the door, not knowing what was going on with her mom when she was ill, is now a beautiful, confident woman. It was the day of the wedding. My mother, my sister and I all dressed up. Together with some snacks, chocolates and even champagne, we made ourselves comfortable and watched this great event on Skype. Definitely not the same as being there, but it was the next best thing, and certainly helped a lot.

I can't describe the emotions I went through while watching my daughter walking down the aisle with Jeremy "giving her away". I am so grateful for what he and Connie had sown into her life. I will always remember and thank them for that. At the end the tears I shed were tears of joy. I hadn't even met my new son-in-law at that time but I, nevertheless, had so much peace about him.

Nine months later I had my green card, and I could be with them for their firstborn's (Michael-John) birth and be part of this great event. What a gift that it was to be part of all that and to bless him.

# CHAPTER 24

## *In a place of transition*

When my children were small, I made a decision that I'm not going to get old and be boring. I wanted to be creatively busy, enjoying my life.

When I was younger, I did a lot of woodcarving. I decided to take a course in lead glass, making lamps for my children and family. It is hard work but gives me so much satisfaction seeing the end result. My children love it, and they have creative ways to get my creations from South Africa to the USA. In one instance, Marguerite mentioned that she really liked this one little table I made. End of story, she somehow managed to get it into her suitcase. Andy was travelling with her so she had some extra space. When they arrived back home in the USA, Andy could not believe his eyes when a table came out of one of their suitcases!

Since I went to Toronto I have received several prophecies (prophetic in simplest form: hearing from the Lord for others). I learned to hold unto them, seeing them as promises from the Lord. One of the most specific words I received from Ivan and Isabel was: "Expect big things, big changes, *nothing* is going to be the same." I'm at that point of my life now. My whole life is changing!

A few years ago while visiting Andy and Marguerite, a well-known prophet offered to prophecy over me. I was so excited! I knew the Lord was going to speak to me through this man and surely he did' I received several promises from the Lord and also received confirmation of previous words that I had received from Ivan and Isabel. What really touched me was that he, three times, said "don't compare yourself with others". The last time "You always compare yourself with others and fall short" was added. That was so spot on! In the future I learned to be aware of those thoughts and to reject them.

Years ago there was a time when I felt so unworthy, I wanted to go deeper, much deeper with the Lord, but there was something holding me back. I twice went for ministry team training in our church, but every time, just before the last session, I would cancel out—only because of "What will people say if you are on the ministry team? You can't do it, not you!" It left me with such an emptiness that I cannot describe. The Lord has done such a miracle in my life. It gives me great pleasure now to minister to people, to be an instrument of the Father's Love flowing through me to others.

One of the prophetic words, that I received years ago, was that I will be involved in ministry, and it has come to pass. It has been such a privilege and an amazing experience to go with Marguerite on some of her ministry trips, seeing people's lives changed. It is incredible to see brokenness and pain in someone's eyes and then being able to give to them what the Lord has given to me, seeing the power of His love setting them free, lifting them, transforming their lives. Marguerite founded her ministry in 2011, and since then the Lord has opened doors for her globally. Her heart, too, is to see the broken-hearted healed, and she delivers a powerful message of freedom and of God's love.

For many years in the past I struggled, believing that the Lord *could* do what He has promised in His Word. Because my dad had made us promises he could not always fulfill because of circumstances, I was projecting that onto my Heavenly Father. Our earthly fathers are our first picture of "father". It was as if I was looking to Him through someone else's glasses and the view was distorted. Now I can say with Smith Wigglesworth "God said it, I believe it, that settles it!" I learned the importance of meditating on scripture so that it can become part of my life. It is my passion to not only know about Him but also know Him...to walk with Him, to talk to Him...listening to what He is saying to me in my everyday life, while driving, washing the dishes, wherever I go. It is important to know that the Greater One lives inside of me, that the resurrection power of the Holy Spirit is in me (and in every believer). I know He is my constant companion and that He is more than able to handle any situation that may come to my life. That is so amazing!

One day the Holy Spirit showed me something about the letter 'P' - if you have Problems, need Provision or Protection, only go into His Presence and stand on His Promises.

I have a few trees in my garden, in my homeland, with birds making their nests in them. Every afternoon I give them bread, and they are so clever. They know when it is time for an early dinner, and if I'm late, they will come to the door trying to get my attention, making it obvious that I am behind schedule. What is my reaction? I will immediately go and feed them. So many times the Father reminds me—if I am so concerned about the birds, he is so much more concerned about me and my needs. While I'm doing this, I feel His Presence, I just know that He is with me, enjoying being there with me and my little birds.

In my office there is a little note to remind me: what I think of is what I will connect with, and what I connect with will become reality in my life. It sometimes happens that He feels so far away. The only way for me to get back with Him, to come into His Presence, is to start meditating on the Greater One living His life through me. If I focus on His life of love, peace and power everything changes. It is true that when we believe what we carry, we change our outside circumstances.

So many times it happens that I am with people, and, as studies have shown, people speak of the negative most of the time. All they see are the bad things happening. That is all they can talk about. All of a sudden I would feel this heaviness in my spirit. I now have learned to "switch channels" again. I've learned not to be a thermometer, following the temperature in the room, but to be a thermostat, controlling it, focusing on the opposite and on His Presence. It is my choice, which way I want to go, and down the road of darkness is not the way.

I now have five gorgeous grandchildren, Elijah, Noah, Michael-John, Sarah and Sam from Thailand. Andy and Marguerite adopted him as a 12-year-old boy two years ago. And now we have another blessing coming to our family, a granddaughter from Thailand will be with us within the next few months. Sam will now have a sister. We are so exited about it!
I wrote their names on the wall in my bathroom so that when I wash my hands, I can pray for them, speaking a blessing over them. To pray for my children, grandchildren and family is a privilege for me, my gift to them.

I'm in a place of transition from one country to another. My time is divided between the country of my birth and the one in my future. There's a lot of excitement, but emotionally, since I'm not young anymore, it is not so easy. I've been rooted in the land of my forbearers for all my life. But even in this the Lord is so faithful. He gave me the scripture "*If I settle on the far side of the sea, even there Your hand will hold me fast.*" (Ps. 139 : 9, 10).

You can do nothing about your past. I had to let go of all my regrets, disappointments, shame, broken dreams and self-blame. No more choices can be made about the past, other than being open for the Lord to bring healing where healing is needed, in His time. But you can do much today that will determine the outcome of your tomorrows. Jesus is the only One who never fails. He proved it over and over to me.

# CHAPTER 25

## *God is faithful!*

Now, at the end of my story, I can see God's grace has been carrying us through all those years.

There were so many times of hopelessness when it felt as if I had come to the end of the rope. In the natural, I could not face any more tomorrows. But not once did the Lord let us down.

It sometimes happened that I set money aside for something I wanted or needed, and one of my children suddenly would have an unexpected need. Without thinking twice and without any regret I would set aside my need and help them. For them to have their needs met was more important to me than my own. I've now learned to live by Kingdom economy (Malachi 3). Things that would be totally impossible in the natural, are possible with His help. He came to meet my every need; I do my part and He does His part.

Many things that went wrong in the past were about wrong decisions I made: not asking for wisdom, not spending enough time with the Lord, not asking for His direction. I knew Him intellectually, but it was not a heart-to-heart relationship. If Jesus only did what the Father did, why did I not just do the same? The Lord is wonderful, He is amazing and He is faithful...always willing to forgive our sins. To know Him as my loving Heavenly Father, Jesus as my Savior and the Holy Spirit as my strength and comforter are the most precious things in my life!

When I grew up, the Holy Spirit was not often mentioned in our church. But I now know that He is my best Friend. He is the Power of creation living inside of me. No situation is too big for Him. If I should worry about my future, it would be as if I would see a future without Him.

Something very special for me about bedtime is to spend time with Him before I fall asleep. I imagine myself lying in my Heavenly Father's arms, meditating on His Love for me, talking to the Lord before falling asleep. That is so amazing—receiving His love and truth, and also what He says about me as I'm falling asleep!

Not many years back, my life was in chaos, but He filled me with His Peace and His Presence. I am in a new season in my life. In Isaiah, 45:2 He promises that He will always be with me and guide me.

# CHAPTER 26

## I have a voice

*Jesus said:*
*"The thief does not come except to steal, and to kill, and to destroy. I have come that they may have life, and that they may have it more abundantly."* John 10:10

I can only give glory to God for what He has done in my life and is still doing.

Once there was a shy little girl, sitting on her suitcase, waiting alone for the late afternoon passenger train to come—then a teenager who thought she was not good enough and that something was wrong with her—then an adult who carried a lot of shame and could not stand up for herself.

BUT, there is a God, One who knew the plans He had for her!

Since I did the International Leaders' School of Ministry in Toronto I have received, in several prophecies, words about teaching. Those words birthed faith in my heart. The Lord did such a miracle in my life, something that only He could do.

My first teaching experience was when a small church in the Cape Province, South Africa invited me to spend a weekend with them. I had just become the National Coordinator for Catch the Fire in South Africa, and they wanted to know more about the Lord's Presence and the Father's Love. I was surprised, in such a way that my first response was "No, not me! I'm not a preacher!" I was the Coordinator and at the time my first focus was building a National Team and the administration side of it all. But they wouldn't let it go and at last I agreed to go.

Two days before I had to leave, I was sitting at my dining room table, preparing what I was going to say. I was so nervous, wondering how I could get out of this...at the same time I knew I couldn't do that, because they had already booked my flights. The Lord, knowing my heart and my feelings, gave me the scripture *"I will help you speak and will teach you what to say"*. Ex.4:12 (NIV)

I started meditating on it, and eventually I had peace to go. I was so desperate for the Holy Spirit; without Him there was no way I could go. I was very thankful that it was in Afrikaans, my mother tongue, and not in English!

So I went. It turned out to be a wonderful weekend, people were touched and their hearts changed. I shared what the Lord laid on my heart and then prayed for people as He led me. The Lord deeply touched their hearts. The pastor wrote a letter saying that they will be forever thankful for what the Lord had done during our time together. The time with them was an incredible breakthrough for me as well! I received revelation that I only need to be available; I'm His vessel. It truly is all about Him. It is His Power flowing through us. We need to make room for Him. He wants to touch people's lives and as we give, we also receive.

Paul said *"My message and my preaching were not with wise and persuasive words but with a demonstration of the Spirit's power."* 1 Cor 2:4. Apart from the Catch the Fire events, there were more opportunities. Not once did the Holy Spirit let me down. Not once did He not come through for me. Every time, I have been just amazed about what He has done in my life, what He is still doing. Thank you Holy Spirit!

The Lord opened doors for me to be part of a medical outreach team in the Philippines, where I was able to minister with Marguerite. What really impacted my life was this one night during prayer ministry time as I was holding a young girl. She was releasing incredible pain. It was so precious to see what the Lord was doing in her and also in many other lives during this trip, and to be aware of the Lord's love flowing through me into people's lives. We ministered in several areas of the country.

I ministered with Marguerite in Germany. Watching my daughter, once a farm girl with no idea of a future like this, is a testimony of the plans our Lord has for us. I was very nervous, even more so because there would be a translator. The moment I started, the precious Holy Spirit took over, and I enjoyed sharing with the people. After Marguerite's teaching, we prayed with them and I felt so connected with them. Many people received emotional and physical healing. People did not want to go home. People from different churches in the area stayed until late at night, to the surprise of the host church pastor. Afterwards they told us that they didn't even expect the people from other churches to come to the event.

From there we went to France, Turkey and Cyprus. Many were set free from pain and hurt of the past. In Turkey I had the privilege to pray for women that came from countries where they are severely persecuted for their faith. Most of them experienced incredible abuse...hard even to talk about. At first I felt so unqualified to minister to people like this. But as we started to pray for them, the Holy Spirit directed us, and many received incredible breakthrough and healing spiritually, emotionally and physically. Yet again, I was able to give away what He has given me. How amazing is His grace. Growing up, I couldn't even dream about helping people on this level. In God, all things are possible. He is just looking for people to come to Him and He will take whatever has happened in their past and turn it into something beautiful. The Cross is the place of Divine Exchange!

Maybe parts of my story sound familiar to you. Or

maybe you've gotten in touch with some emotions while reading my book. Know that Jesus paid the ultimate price for your freedom, just as He did for mine. Simply come to Him. Just as you are. No performance. Bring your life to Him. If you have not given your life to Him, or maybe you thought you knew Him but you realize now that you only know Him intellectually, not in your heart, you can pray this prayer:

*Jesus, thank you for what You have done for me on the Cross. I repent for all my sins and ask Your forgiveness. (share your heart with Him). Jesus I ask You to come into my heart. I give my life to You. Thank you that I am now Yours. Amen.*

Jesus is the way to the Father. He said He is the truth, the way and the life. No one comes to the Father except through Him. Then, it doesn't stop at salvation. Jesus is the way to our Father and He is waiting for you. So just come to Him and forgive every authority figure, every father figure in your life that misrepresented "Father", and give them a gift of forgiveness, just as you received your gift of forgiveness. Share your heart with your Heavenly Father. This is a process, a journey, not a one-off moment. Repent where you have judged them. Ask the Father to reveal to you who He is as the perfect Father. Ask the Holy Spirit to fill you, so that you can know Him for who He truly is. Jesus said the Holy Spirit is our Helper and for us to have communion with Him, yes, to share with Him. Get to know Him. Remember the Holy Spirit is the Power that raised Jesus from the dead and He is now inside of you. When you share and pray for people, remember that He is with you and His Presence inside of you touches those around you. Enjoy the journey.

*In the Name of Jesus I bless you with the Love, the Joy and the Peace of the Lord. I bless you to know Jesus in the fullness of who He is. I bless you to know your Heavenly Father as the perfect Father who is for you and wants the best for you. I bless you with His Provision and Protection. I bless you with a long and fruitful life. And I bless you as a resting place of the Holy Spirit! Amen*